THE
RENDLESHAM
FOREST UFO
CONSPIRACY

Published by Lisa Hagan Books 2020

www.lisahaganbooks.com

Powered by

SHADOW
TEAMS

Cover design and interior layout by Simon Hartshorne

THE
RENDLESHAM
FOREST UFO
CONSPIRACY

A Close Encounter
Exposed as a Top Secret
Government Experiment

NICK REDFERN

CONTENTS

INTRODUCTION

In the final days of December 1980, multiple strange encounters and wild incidents occurred in Rendlesham Forest, Suffolk, England. And across a period of three nights, no less. Based upon their personal encounters, many of those who were present believed something almost unbelievable came down in the near-pitch-black woods on the night of December 26. Lives were altered forever – and for the most part not for the better, I need to stress. Many of those who were present on those fantastic nights found their minds dazzled, tossed and turned – and incredibly quickly, too. Those incidents involved American military personnel who, at the time it all happened, were stationed in the United Kingdom. Their primary role was to provide significant support in the event the Soviets decided to flex their muscles just a little bit too much – or, worse still, planned on hitting the proverbial red button and ending civilization in hours. Maybe, even in minutes.

Reportedly, those U.S. personnel who were in the area and helped to protect the U.K., came face to face with something much stranger than the likes of a crashed Soviet satellite, a secret Stealth-type plane that malfunctioned and went off-course, or something similar to today's drones – all of which have been suggested as potential candidates for the whatever-it-was that landed four decades ago. Some, though, are absolutely certain that unearthly entities were encountered: *aliens from another world.*

It's fair to say that when it comes to UFOs, Rendlesham Forest is right up there with the Roswell "UFO crash" of July 1947. It's no wonder at all that the case has become known as "Britain's Roswell." Not because anything actually crashed in the forest – it was described as being much more like a touch-down – but because of the widespread visibility and notoriety that surrounds the case. The December 1980 encounters have been the subjects of countless prime-time television documentaries on both sides of the pond, and of more than a few books, too. Mostly, the authors behind those same books take the view extraterrestrials really *did* come down in picturesque Suffolk – and not on just one occasion. More than a few of the military personnel involved have come forward to tell their stories of what happened. Some of them are sure they had encounters with extraterrestrials. For them, no other answer can be considered. What if, however, there is another explanation for what happened four decades ago? And what if that explanation, if revealed, would prove to be *even more* controversial than the notion that extraterrestrials really manifested within our very midst? The ramifications for the field of Ufology could be – and likely will be - immense.

The questions get even more inflammatory: were U.S. Air Force personnel subjected to mind-bending technology of a terrestrial – rather than of an extraterrestrial – nature? Was the whole thing really a series of top-secret experiments of American intelligence, U.K. intelligence, scientists and military agencies? Was the entire, wretched thing initiated to see how – and to what extent – the minds of targeted individuals could be manipulated and to the point where the witnesses would believe just about anything? Even to the point of convincing some airmen that aliens had appeared and, maybe, even communicated with us? Yes. Were human rights waved away for reasons relative to national security? Without a doubt. Did both the U.S. and the U.K. governments engage in high-level cover-ups and conspiracies to hide the bizarre and frightening truth behind the legend? Those questions, and many more, are the ones I tackle and answer in the pages of the book you're getting into right now.

There is an overwhelming problem when it comes to the matter of trying to solve the U.K.'s most famous alien affair. So many UFO researchers, and some of the eyewitnesses too, have catastrophically failed to realize something deeply important. It's the fact the stories of down-to-earth cover-ups and conspiracies concerning the case are far more plausible than anything that Ufology has, thus far, ever been able to successfully bring to the table. Until now, that is. And that's not my ego going into overdrive. It just so happens to be the truth. The failure to appreciate and understand the real picture was – and still is – due to a *yearning need* on the part of so many saucer-seekers to conclude that aliens landed in the U.K. four decades ago. It's primarily down to what certain players *want* to hear, rather than what they *should* hear. So many UFO researchers have flown the flag of the extraterrestrial theory for Rendlesham for years but have not paid significant attention to what, in many ways, is a much bigger story. If all of this sounds critical, well, it is. And it's meant to be. It's wake-up time.

There's another matter, too: Rendlesham is – and particularly so from the E.T. perspective - a definitive "cash cow." There is an old-but-famous saying: "There's gold in them thar hills." There are also wads of dollars in those woods, if you get my somewhat cynical drift. Saying what so many people *want* to hear about Rendlesham is guaranteed to sell books. And most people in Ufology *want* Rendlesham to be an extraterrestrial event; that is a reality. No one, however, can accuse me of saying what the UFO research community desires to hear. I guarantee that the vast majority of people reading this book will *not* be happy with what they learn in the pages ahead. They *should*, however, take a careful look at all of the material that awaits them. After reading *The Rendlesham Forest UFO Conspiracy*, your views on the truth behind the 1980 encounters may change – and change radically. Maybe, though, the belief systems of some are so embedded those same beliefs will overwhelm common-sense. If that is the case, they probably won't thank me for telling this story. They *will*, at least, know the truth that has been successfully hidden for such a long time. And how all of us have been deceived and manipulated. And how amazingly easy it was all to achieve.

Like it or like it not, I'm going to put the truth into perspective and reveal to you the *real* picture of what went on in that famous forest. Not the exciting tales of alien-human interaction, but the disturbing and secret operations of scientists and military officers who ran wild and who were willing to manipulate minds, and screw the cost to those who were severely affected by what they saw. Minds were not just manipulated: those same minds were damaged, too.

The real data on the Forest farrago is out there: all to be found; just waiting. That is, if one knows how and where to find it. Most importantly, how to interpret it and finally accept it for what it is. Sadly, so many of the "I want to believe" crowd don't want to know or hear about the likes of military experiments, amazing holograms, mind-manipulation, and hallucinogens – all of which, you'll soon find out, are part and parcel of the story that is about to explode. What so many people *do* want, however, are their black-eyed, large-headed, dwarfish creatures from a planet that's far away. Too bad: there's none of that here.

I should stress that this book is not intended to scrutinize every single claim and observation pertaining to the Rendlesham story. Such a thing would result in the publication of a book close to 1,000 pages in length, maybe even more. Rather, my story is designed to make a solid case pertaining to the bleakest of all scenarios - and then present it to you, the readers, for debate and discussion. It's the theory that no-one wants to hear, but it *is* the theory that everybody is most certainly going to get.

With my semi-rant now over, it's finally time for me to present the dark and dirty truth of the Rendlesham Forest incident of December 1980 and unveil it for what it was and what it still is: a complete and utter, outrageous scandal. And it has ZERO to do with extraterrestrials. It's much worse than little green men from the stars could ever be.

1

"THE OBJECT WAS HOVERING OR ON LEGS"

Situated in the county of Suffolk, England, Rendlesham Forest is just like about any other large area of woodland. It's a place that provokes a sense of tranquility and a feeling of relaxation – but also, at times, an air of distinct, quiet eeriness. Deer, foxes and badgers run freely through the forest. The woods are filled with the inviting chirping of birds, such as buzzards, red kites and nightjars. This particular forest, however – it runs to more than 1,400 acres, and is largely comprised of Corsican and Scots pine trees - can boast of being somewhat different to most forests; in fact, it's almost unique. You know why.

The forest itself sits adjacent to what used to be the United States / Royal Air Force complexes of Bentwaters-Woodbridge. Personnel at both bases played significant roles in the Second World War to help defeat the Nazis. Without the American presence it's almost certain that Hitler and his collective scum would have overwhelmed the U.K. In the aftermath of the war, and particularly so when the Cold War began, the bases continued to retain their strategic and important position in the country. Until their closure in 1993, Woodbridge and Bentwaters both served as front-line defenders of the U.K.'s security. At their peak there were more than 13,000 U.S. service-personnel at the twin facilities. Rumor has it – but has never been fully confirmed – that a sizeable number of nuclear weapons were held there for an unclear period of years. In addition, several thousand American military personnel lived off base, in rented cottages and houses scattered throughout the welcoming communities of Woodbridge, Alderburgh, Wickham Market and more.

No one knew that one day, the area – and particularly a large woodland at the heart of this story - would become famous all across the world. Incredibly, though, that is precisely what occurred.

"THE OBJECTS MOVED RAPIDLY IN SHARP, ANGULAR MOVEMENTS"

To understand exactly what occurred in the woods on those fateful nights, it's important that we go back to the beginning: (a) the events themselves; and (b) a near-legendary memo on the incidents that was carefully prepared by Lieutenant Colonel Charles Halt. At the time, he was the Deputy Base Commander at RAF Bentwaters. On January 13, 1981, Halt prepared the following report; it was sent to the U.K. Ministry of Defense (MoD) for scrutiny. It gives a fairly brief – but certainly detailed – account of what happened:

1. Early in the morning of 27 Dec 80 (approximately 0300L) two USAF security police patrolmen saw unusual lights outside the back gate at RAF Woodbridge. Thinking an aircraft might have crashed or been forced down, they called for permission to go outside the gate to investigate. The on-duty flight chief responded and allowed three patrolmen to proceed on foot. The individuals reported

seeing a strange glowing object in the forest. The object was described as being metallic in appearance and triangular in shape, approximately two to three meters across the base and approximately two meters high. It illuminated the entire forest with a white light. The object itself had a pulsing red light on top and a bank(s) of blue lights underneath. The object was hovering or on legs. As the patrolmen approached the object, it maneuvered through the trees and disappeared. At this time the animals on a nearby farm went into a frenzy. The object was briefly sighted approximately an hour later near the back gate.

2. The next day, three depressions 1.5 inches deep and 7 inches in diameter were found where the object had been sighted on the ground. The following night (29 Dec 80) the area was checked for radiation. Beta/gamma readings of 0.1 milliroentgens were recorded with peak readings in the three depressions and near the center of the triangle formed by the depressions. A nearby tree had moderate (0.05–0.07) readings on the side of the tree toward the depressions.

3. Later in the night a red sun-like light was seen through the trees. It moved about and pulsed. At one point it appeared to throw off glowing particles and then broke into five separate white objects and then disappeared. Immediately thereafter, three star-like objects were noticed in the sky, two objects to the north and one to the south, all of which were about 10 degrees off the horizon. The objects moved rapidly in sharp, angular movements and displayed red, green and blue lights. Objects to the north appeared to be elliptical through an 8-12 power lens. They

then turned to full circles. Objects to the north remained in the sky for an hour or more. The object to the south was visible for two or three hours and beamed down a stream of light from time to time. Numerous individuals, including the undersigned, witnessed the activities in paragraphs 2 and 3.

Charles I. Halt, Lt Col, USAF
Deputy Base Commander

TESTIMONY FROM THE MEN WHO WERE THERE

There is far more to the encounters than the content of a one-page piece of paper - *way more*, in fact. Much of it was left out of Halt's three-paragraph memo, as we'll see. Two of the most important and credible figures in this entire story are John Burroughs and Jim Penniston. Burroughs was in the U.S. Air Force for more than a quarter of a century, working in law enforcement. As for Penniston, he entered the USAF in 1973. At the time all hell broke loose in Rendlesham Forest, Penniston was a Senior Security Officer. Both men had startling encounters in those December nights. Penniston actually touched the whatever-it-was; something that he now believes caused him to receive a binary code message that was, essentially, downloaded into his mind.

Techopedia explains what, precisely, binary codes are: "Binary code is the most simplistic form of data. It is represented entirely by a binary system of digits consisting of a string of consecutive zeros and ones. Binary code is often associated with machine code in that binary sets can be combined to form raw code, which is interpreted by a computer or other piece of hardware."

PAST, PRESENT AND FUTURE

In a May 6, 2018 article for the *Mysterious Universe* website, and titled "Aliens: Us From a Future Time," I wrote: "Formerly of the U.S. Air Force, and one of the key military players in the famous UFO encounter at Rendlesham Forest, Suffolk, England in December 1980, Sergeant Jim Penniston – in 1994 – underwent hypnotic regression, as part of an attempt to try and recall deeply buried data relative to what occurred to him during one of Britain's closest encounters. Very interestingly, and while under hypnosis, Penniston stated that our presumed aliens are, in reality, visitors from a far-flung future. That future, Penniston added, is very dark, in infinitely deep trouble, polluted and where the Human Race is overwhelmingly blighted by reproductive problems. The answer to those same massive problems, Penniston was told by the entities he met in the woods, is that they travel into the distant past – to our present day – to secure sperm, eggs and chromosomes, all as part of an effort to try and ensure the continuation of the severely waning Human Race of tomorrow."

"I FOUND MYSELF TALKING AND TALKING"

Ian Ridpath, a skeptic of the UFO story, said: "In the days following the events of December 26 and 28, Halt and Penniston were debriefed separately by [Colonel] Ted Conrad, Halt's boss. These were the only two witnesses Conrad talked to. It is sometimes claimed in UFO circles that the witnesses were subjected to interrogation by the Air Force Office of Special Investigations (AFOSI), including injections by the so-called 'truth drug' sodium pentothal." In January 2010, however, Conrad denied drugs were used.

UFO researcher Dr. David Clarke was told by Conrad: "There were no conspiracies, no secret operation, no missile accident, and no harsh interrogations by OSI. I was in a position to know about the OSI. They had their own chain of command, but in practice the OSI commander kept me informed of any ongoing investigations they had."

Taking into consideration the fact that much of the story in this book deals with hallucinogens, drugs, and mind-changing substances (as you shall soon come to see), I see no reason at all why we should dismiss the words of Penniston. He was on-site and a dedicated member of the U.S. military. In fact, I think we should take Penniston's words to be the gospel truth – *as he saw it*.

In terms of what "truth drugs" are, and what they actually do to the mind, there are these important words from the *Science History Institute*: "No other truth drug had as successful a run as scopolamine, but many others were given a try. Sketchy intelligence and press reports in the 1940s and 1950s suggested the Chinese and Russians were experimenting not just with scopolamine but also with amphetamines, such as Benzedrine, and barbiturates, such as sodium thiopental (also known as Sodium Pentothal). In one such account, Lieutenant John Ori, an American, said he found a sweet white powder in his food while detained in a prison camp during the Korean War. After eating, 'I found myself talking and talking,' he told a journalist. 'I was hardly able to control what I was saying. I talked a blue streak.'"

As for John Burroughs, while recalling one particular incident in the woods, he said that "we had a blue transparent light come streaking towards us." Burroughs said Sergeant Adrian Bustinza – who also had close-up encounters - "went down to the ground." And that Bustinza watched Burroughs "go into" that same light. Burroughs added that Bustinza "saw me disappear." Incredibly, Burroughs added that Bustinza "saw the light explode and I was gone for several minutes before I reappeared. I have no recall of it."

We'll return to all three men – Bustinza, Penniston and Burroughs – later.

RUMORS, INVESTIGATIONS, AND A
DEDICATED TEAM OF THREE

On the issue of how Ufology learned of the story, there's no doubt at all it was the team of Brenda Butler, Dot Street and Jenny Randles who got the ball rolling. They were the authors of the very first book on the mystery, *Sky Crash*, which was published in 1984. There is also no doubt that without their combined investigations, our knowledge of the incidents would be nowhere compared to where we are today. Possibly, even, without those three persistent investigators the truth behind those incidents would have remained hidden and locked away. Forever? I would not bet against it. That gives you some idea of the depth and determination of Dot, Jenny and Brenda to get the answers.

A bit of background for you on how the story began to surface: Brenda lived not at all far from the forest and had more than a few contacts in the region. Notably, that included friends who were employees of the U.S. military. It wasn't one hundred percent inevitable that Brenda would hear tales of something strange having taken place just outside the confines of RAF Woodbridge. It was, however, highly likely that such a thing would eventually occur. And as the history books have shown, such a thing *did* occur. Dot and Brenda were friends and decided to take a deep and careful look at the story. Jenny Randles joined their team soon after, in early 1981. The three were soon hot on the trail of the story – and barely a month after Lieutenant Colonel Halt had put his memo together for the U.K.'s Ministry of Defense. And, the three never looked back. It was a story that suggested, just maybe, a spacecraft from a faraway world had come down in the woods. In the world of Ufology, this was a development that could not have been envisaged just a short period earlier.

AN IMPORTANT INFORMANT

One of the key sources for the story who the three women relied on - and whose unforgettable words galvanized the trio to look ever deeper into the story - was the pseudonymous "Steve Roberts." Such was the sensitivity surrounding the man and his story, he was careful to mask his real name. A lot of water has gone under the bridge since the very early part of 1981, however. Today, we know so much more. That includes the real name of that prime early source.

Gary Heseltine is a former Royal Air Force Police officer who went on to have a twenty-four-year-long career with the British Transport Police, serving the majority of the time as a detective. Heseltine, who has spent a large amount of time studying what happened in Rendlesham Forest, says: "Surprisingly to this day, many people don't realize that the mysterious 'Steve Roberts witness' has been identified for many years as J. D. Ingles. Ingles was on the base at the time of the incident, a Sergeant in the Reports and Analysis section of the 81st Security Police Squadron."

THE INVESTIGATION STARTS TO GROW
AND THE MOD GETS DISTURBED

It was, to a large degree, the words of their source that caught the attention of Street, Butler and Randles. They did a very good, solid job of pursuing the story. It was soon published. *Sky Crash* makes for fascinating reading. Shadowy characters, Ministry of Defense chicanery, sinister goings-on in the woods, tales of extraterrestrial visitation, and military figures hiding their real names for fear of what might happen to them, were just the start of things. In the weeks and months that followed, the Ministry of Defense proved to be highly close-mouthed when it came to discussing the December incidents with members of the public and the media. No surprise. They were even more cautious about chatting with an energized team of UFO sleuths who weren't going to give up. That's Jenny, Dot and Brenda, of course.

In some ways, the MoD was unable to do very much about it, as wild rumors of the startling events were already seeping out. Eventually matters would develop into a chaotic torrent. To demonstrate how incredibly careful and determined the MoD was to try and keep matters under wraps, it was not until April 13, 1983 that an official admission was made to Jenny Randles that a handful of "lights" had been seen in the vicinity of Rendlesham Forest and remained "unexplained." That's right: *two years* passed before the rumors of something very strange and non-human having been seen in Rendlesham Forest began to unravel in the world of intelligence and the military. Those who were hiding the truth were now in the dangerous position of losing control of the situation.

Almost two months later to the day, a copy of Lieutenant Colonel Halt's memo was declassified in accordance with the laws of the U.S. Freedom of Information Act. It was provided to a now-deceased American UFO investigator, Robert Todd. In a June 14, 1983 letter to Todd, Colonel Peter Bent – who, at the time, was the Commander of the 513th Combat Support Group (CSG) – made an amazement statement. He said: "It might interest you to know that the U.S. Air Force had no longer retained a copy of the 13 January 1981 letter written by Lt. Col. Charles I. Halt. The Air Force file copy had been properly disposed of in accordance with Air Force regulations. Fortunately, through diligent inquiry and the gracious consent of Her Majesty's government, the British

Ministry of Defense and the Royal Air Force, the U.S. Air Force was provided with a copy for you."

It wasn't long at all before Brenda, Dot and Jenny found themselves in a runaround. Curiously, during the course of an interview with MoD spokeswoman Pam Titchmarsh on August 18, 1983, Randles was told that – contrary to the statement made by Colonel Bent – the Ministry of Defense had *not* supplied the Americans with a copy of Halt's memorandum. Notably, Titchmarsh was very wary about discussing the case with Randles, who had made a trip down to London with Street and Butler. "I wouldn't know," was Titchmarsh's uneasy and succinct reply when Randles asked her if the MoD's "operational staff" had built up their own files on the case.

Nevertheless, since a copy of the Halt memo had been released to Robert Todd by U.S. authorities, Titchmarsh was – at the *very* least - obliged to admit her department in the MoD (Defense Secretariat 8) did have a copy of Halt's report on file. Despite that, the Ministry of Defense denied the events of December 1980 were of any kind of defense significance. It was a stubborn, mule-like stance from which the Ministry of Defense has never, ever wavered. The MoD just loves that mule. Always has, always will.

AN AMAZING PIECE OF EVIDENCE APPEARS

Roughly one year after Pam Titchmarsh admitted to Jenny Randles that Lieutenant Colonel Halt's one-page memorandum *was* on file, a copy of an audio-tape recording made within Rendlesham Forest - when the primary activity occurred - surfaced. Lasting for approximately eighteen minutes, the recording is basically a running (and stunning) commentary attesting to the accuracy of Halt's typed report to the MoD in January 1981. The reader should note that the eighteen minutes of recorded data actually covers a period of several hours. Nevertheless, we are still left with a vital source of corroborating evidence for the events detailed in paragraphs two and three of the Halt memo. Salient extracts from the recording follow:

HALT: It's a strange, small red light, looks to be maybe a quarter to a half-mile, maybe further out.

HALT: The light's still there and all the barnyard animals have gone quiet now. We're heading about 110, 120 degrees from the site out through to the clearing now, still getting a reading on the meter…Everywhere else is just deathly calm. There is no doubt about it: there's some type of strange flashing red light ahead.

HALT: We see strange strobe-like flashes to the, er, well, they're sporadic, but there's definitely some kind of phenomenon. At about ten degrees, horizon, directly north, we've got two strange objects, er, half-moon shape, dancing about with colored lights on 'em. That, er, guess to be about five to ten miles out, maybe less. The half-moons are now turning to full circles, as though there was an eclipse or something there, for a minute or two…One's moving away from us.

SERGEANT MONROE NEVELS: It's moving out fast.

MASTER SERGEANT BOBBY BALL: This one on the right's heading away too.

HALT: Now we're observing what appears to be a beam coming down to the ground. This is unreal. And the objects are still in the sky, although the one to the south looks like it's losing a little bit of altitude. The object to the south looks like it's losing a little bit of altitude. The object to the south is still beaming down lights to the ground.

HALT: Okay, we're looking at the thing; we're probably about two or three hundred yards away. It looks like an eye winking at you. It's still moving from side to side, and when you put the starscope [Author's note: basically, night-vision] on it, it sort of has a hollow center; a dark center. It's, you know, like the pupil of an eye looking at you, winking. And the flash is so bright to the starscope that it almost burns your eye. We passed the farmer's house and crossed into the next field, and now we have multiple sightings, of lights with a similar shape and all. But, they seem to be steady, now, rather than a pulsating or glow with a red flash.

HALT: At 0244 we're at the far side of the farmer's – second farmer's – field. And made sighting again, about 110 degrees. This looks like it's clear out to the coast; its right on the horizon. Moves about a bit, and flashes from time to time…We're turning around, heading back towards the base. The object to the south is still beaming down lights to the ground. 0400 hours, one object still hovering over Woodbridge base at about five degrees off the horizon, still moving erratic.

HALT: The object to the south is still beaming down lights to the ground. One object still hovering over Woodbridge base at about five to ten degrees off the horizon, still moving erratic and similar lights and beaming down as earlier.

There are two very important areas that pertain to Halt's recording that need to be stressed. First, the transcript fails to get across to the reader – but most certainly not to the listener – the sheer states of excitement and anxiety exhibited in the voices of those men who were in the woods. Second, there is the matter of the length of the recording versus the actual amount of time the men were in the woods. Halt explained and clarified this issue in a 2008 episode of the popular – but now defunct – TV show, *UFO Hunters*. He said: "The tapes are twenty minutes in duration, so there's no way I could have kept the tape running the whole time. I must have stopped that tape a hundred times. I was going click-click-click-click the whole time we were out there because I didn't want to run out of tape."

More revelations surfaced: In 1984, *Clear Intent*, a book written by UFO investigators Lawrence Fawcett and Barry J. Greenwood, was published. It contained six pages of material that added even more to the Rendlesham story, such as claims of the confiscation of radar tapes, of "a metallic craft and entities seen in a clearing at Rendlesham" and a scenario almost akin to the final stages of Steven Spielberg's 1977 hit-movie, *Close Encounters of the Third Kind*.

Jenny Randles' *From Out of the Blue* book surfaced in 1991. It revealed the then-most-recent data pertaining to the case, as well as a number of theories that suggested the Bentwaters-Woodbridge incidents may not have involved aliens. Randles addressed such possibilities as a "nuclear accident," a "secret mini-helicopter," a "stealth jet," and a drone or a missile that had "gone berserk." Randles said: "Not all of these could possibly have been correct and very likely none of them were."

Jenny was right: none of those theories were the correct one. We'll soon come to the truth of it all.

MEETING THE MINISTRY

The majority of the staff at the MoD who handled the UFO subject – Pam Titchmarsh being a good example – were decidedly cagey when it came to the matter of getting chummy and chatty with Ufologists. Matters began to change for the better in 1991. That was when a man named Nick Pope took over the reins in "the UFO office." He was refreshingly open – to the extent he could. So, on March 29, 1994, I decided to be proactive. I took a trip to London and had a face-to-face chat with Pope in a nearby bar. We found a quiet area where I could record the interview, got our cold beers, and began. Nick began by explaining to me funding for the MoD office – for UFO investigations - was tiny in the extreme. In Pope's own words: "There is no specific 'UFO budget,' excepting the staff costs, i.e. around twenty percent of my salary, together with a tiny percentage of some other salaries, reflecting my line management's supervisory role."

And that was it. Even the U.S. Air Force's *Project Blue Book* had a bigger budget - and that, back in the 1950s and 1960s, was hardly what one could call astronomical. On top of that, Pope quite openly told me that he *never* went out of the MoD building to undertake an in-the-field-type investigation: he would simply sit at his desk and take phone-calls or handle letters from UFO witnesses and flying saucer investigators. The reports would then be sent to an arm of Defense Intelligence for scrutiny and explanations. It was hardly like the exciting scenarios we saw when *The X-Files* began, which was just one year before I met Pope. And, tragically, there wasn't even a single Dana Scully lookalike anywhere in sight. The good news, however, was that Nick Pope was quite willing to chat and share what he could with me about Rendlesham. Pope said the following to me:

DISCUSSING UFOS AT THE MINISTRY OF DEFENSE

"The sighting, of course, occurred in 1980, but as far as I've been able to tell, our papers pretty much start following a *News of the World* report [Note: the *NotW* was a very popular U.K. tabloid newspaper that closed in 2011, as a result of a major scandal that toppled the long-running publication]. I've not been able to turn up where we originally received [Halt's report] which came under a covering note from Squadron Leader David Moreland, the RAF Base Commander. I've not been able to turn up the letter Squadron Leader Moreland wrote, nor have I been able to turn up anything that indicates what we did, when, and if we received it in December 1980 or early in eighty-one."

Pope continued: "I'm aware from the file that's built up since, that the incident was looked at in the same time and was judged to be of no defense significance, but I don't have many more details than that. It's not disputed, I don't think, that something strange was seen there by Colonel Halt and by some of the other personnel. What's obviously in dispute is what it was. And I know that although some people have some more exotic theories, there was a chap who put forward the theory it was simply Orford Ness lighthouse reflected through the trees and all sorts of lights and shadows as a result of that."

"THE TRAIL HAD GONE COLD"

What this means is that Pope, the presumed number-one figure in the MoD's UFO project (if you can call it a project), didn't know much at all about Rendlesham Forest, despite running the UFO side of things since 1991. In 1994, when I interviewed Nick, one could learn much more about the events from reading some of the various books on the subject of Rendlesham - such as *Sky*

Crash and *From Out of the Blue* – instead of perusing the MoD's apparently vague file. The "chap" who Pope hazily referred to is Ian Ridpath, the author of, among other books, *Stars and Planets Guide* and the *Oxford Dictionary of Astronomy*.

Also, when we talked about the matter of Lieutenant Colonel Halt's audio,, Pope yet again demonstrated his lack of knowledge on the case. He said of the tape issue: "UFO researchers talk about it a lot. My initial opinion was that I thought that that was a fake, but I understand since then Colonel Halt was asked directly about it and said that the tape is a genuine recording. My problem with all this is that I joined Sec (AS) 2a [the office in which Pope worked] in 1991, some ten years-plus after this had all taken place. With all the best will in the world, the trail had gone cold. By then there was very little I could do except look at the file of correspondence which, as I say, pretty much kicked off after the *News of the World* article, so it's been a very difficult case for me to form an opinion on.

"One of the main reasons that I thought the tape was a fake was, I found it a bit difficult to imagine the concept of people actually going out to investigate something in guard duty and having a recorder and pressing 'Play' in the first place; I found it a slightly bizarre concept. I try to stay open-minded on it. The problem is that, as with most UFO cases, unless you solve them very quickly and get to speak to the people straight away, the trail goes cold."

I asked Pope what, exactly, was contained in the file he had access to. His reply was: "It's simply a correspondence file. What we don't have is anything that shows what, if any, consideration was given to the case by the MoD at the time in 1980. I'm not even clear it got through to us."

What all of this tells us is that if there *was* a cover-up of the Rendlesham sightings – and I fully believe there was – then Nick

Pope was most certainly not a part of it. There's no doubt on my part that Pope was out of any kind of highly-classified loop concerning the encounters in the woods. Later, we'll see how Pope went on to embrace the Rendlesham case, studied it carefully, and finally revealed some extraordinary data – in a book of his very own: *Encounter in Rendlesham Forest*, published in 2014.

WHEN FILES ON THE WEIRDNESS IN
THE WOODS START TO APPEAR

In 2001, the Ministry of Defense declassified its "Forest File," as I like to call it. Dr. David Clarke, who has spent a great deal of time studying the government's UFO files at the National Archives, wrote of this particular development: "What is clear from the official documents is the MoD's early reluctance to reveal what little it knew about the UFO incidents. [It] allowed the mystery to grow and provided fuel for allegations of cover-ups. In fact it was two decades before the full contents of the MoD's file on the Rendlesham incident were revealed. Early in 2001, with Britain's own Freedom of Information Act pending, the MoD finally released the papers they held on the incident after I applied to see them. They did not contain the 'smoking gun' anticipated by UFOlogists who had speculated about the contents for 20 years. Instead the file revealed a half-hearted investigation by disinterested officials. Most surprising of all, the papers revealed the MoD did not feel it was necessary to interview Halt or any of the airmen involved in the original sightings."

That wasn't quite the end of the matter, however. In 2011, the BBC ran an online article titled "UFO files reveal 'Rendlesham incident' papers missing." The BBC's Neil Henderson wrote: "Intelligence papers on a reported UFO sighting known as the 'Rendlesham incident' have gone missing, files from the National

Archives reveal. The missing files relate to a report of mysterious lights from US servicemen at RAF Woodbridge in Suffolk in 1980. The disappearance came to light with the release of 8,000 previously classified documents on UFOs. Officials found a 'huge' gap where defense intelligence files relating to the case should be, the papers show." The files also referred to a "deliberate attempt" to "eradicate the records covering this incident."

There's no doubt that what really provoked people with an interest in UFOs to sit up - and look and listen carefully - was the publication of three particular books on the incident. They were: Georgina Bruni's *You Can't Tell the People,* published in 2000; 2014's aforementioned *Encounter in Rendlesham Forest,* written by Nick Pope, John Burroughs and Jim Penniston – the latter pair being two of the most important figures in the whole story - and *The Rendlesham Enigma,* written by Jim Penniston himself and Gary Osborn. The latter surfaced in 2019.

Let us now see why I conclude the Rendlesham Forest incidents had not a single solitary thing to do with extraterrestrials, but *everything* to do with high-tech secret experimentation designed to see just how far the human mind could be used and abused.

2

"THE SUBJECT OF FEVERED SPECULATION"

One of the most important revelations in this overall story concerns the locations of where the monumental events happened. I'm actually not talking about Rendlesham Forest. At least, right now I'm not. Rather, I'm talking about the *surrounding* locales and their mysterious histories. And why do I consider it my duty to bring your attention to those same surroundings? I'll tell you: it's vital to note that for decades the *entire area* around those famous woods acted as a powerful magnet for classified government programs, sensitive military operations, and top secret projects. They were all of a highly important – but down to earth and domestic – nature.

On January 28, 1935, the Tizard Committee, established under the directorship of Sir Henry Tizard, convened its first meeting. It ultimately led to the top-secret development of a workable radar system of the type employed in the Second World War. In an article titled "The Tizard Mission and the Development of the Atomic Bomb," David Zimmerman says: "In August 1940 Sir Henry Tizard led a group of British scientists and technical experts to North America. Over the next four months, the members of the Tizard or British Technical Mission undertook one of the greatest transfers of technical and scientific information in history. In over 150 meetings with American military, technical, and scientific experts the mission provided almost all of Great Britain's military technical secrets to the United States. The United States reciprocated in kind."

Most pertinent of all to this book, much of that highly classified research was conducted at Bawdsey Manor on the Deben Estuary. It's just north of the town of Felixstowe, and a mere stone's throw from what were, for so many years, the military bases of Royal Air Force Bentwaters and Royal Air Force Woodbridge.

"HE WAS CALLED OUT TO PICK UP DEAD BODIES"

To understand the wider scope of this part of the story, we must address one of the strangest – and one of the most enduring - stories from the Second World War. Arguably, it has become a legend; a most grim and grisly one, too. It concerns a small village in Suffolk called Shingle Street. It is located in between the aforementioned Bawdsey and Orford. As the *Guardian* newspaper says: "Shingle Street itself has been the subject of fevered speculation ever since it was evacuated in 1940. Conspiracies include rumors of a German landing and a shoreline littered with burning bodies, schemes to protect the coastline with an impenetrable barrage of flames and the testing of experimental chemical bombs. Four dead German airmen were certainly washed up on the beach, and weapons testing did result in the *Lifeboat Inn* being blown up. As for the rest, the conspiracy theories rumble on."

The BBC, too, has addressed the matter of what did, or what *didn't*, happen at Shingle Street all those decades ago: "A World War II mystery over a 'failed Nazi invasion' at a remote beach in Suffolk may have been manufactured by Britain's head of propaganda, a BBC documentary suggests. The BBC *East Inside Out* team investigated the events of 1940 at Shingle Street. The program suggested that Sefton Delmer, a former *Daily Express* journalist who – during the Second World War - organized Britain's 'black' propaganda unit, could have spread rumors of a failed Nazi invasion to boost morale. The rumors may have even been used to cover up the loss of lives on a British naval destroyer. Since 1940 there have been continuing rumors of a sea on fire and a failed invasion attempt at Shingle Street, *near Woodbridge, Suffolk* [italics mine]. Mike Paintin said that his father, a soldier during World War II, told how he was called out to pick up dead bodies from Shingle Street. 'My father and the rest of his colleagues were called out to pull bodies from the sea,' he said. 'The common link was that they were all in German uniforms and were all badly burned.'"

Then, just a few years later – specifically in 1943 – much of Rendlesham Forest was cleared to allow for the construction of the highly strategic RAF Woodbridge. The forest suffered even more devastation on October 15-16, 1987. That was when a huge amount of damage was caused to the woods: they, and significant other parts of the U.K., were hit by the almost unfathomable power of a massive, destructive cyclone. I was working and living in Harlow, Essex, England at the time, as a van-driver, and got to see the terrible destruction up close. It took years for the forest to recover.

CLASSIFIED PROGRAMS

We'll now take a look at a place called Orford Ness and what went happened there in the 1950s. The U.K.'s National Trust state: "The 1950s saw the construction of specialized facilities to exploit new post-war technologies such as nuclear power. AWRE [Atomic Weapons Research Establishment] Orford Ness was one of only a few sites in the U.K., and indeed the world, where purpose-built facilities were created for testing the components of nuclear weapons. At the height of the Cold War AWRE and the Royal Aircraft Establishment used Orford Ness for developmental work on the atomic bomb."

Moving onto the 1960s, there is the following from the National Trust: "In 1968 work started on the top secret Anglo-American System 441A 'over-the-horizon' (OTH) backscatter radar project, finally code-named 'Cobra Mist.' The Anglo-American project, whose main contractor was the Radio Corporation of America, was set up to carry out several 'missions.' including detection and tracking of aircraft, detection of missile and satellite vehicle launchings, fulfilling intelligence requirements and providing a research and development test-bed…"

We're still not done with the classified, government programs in the area.

A MYSTERIOUS DEATH – ONE OF MANY

From the early 1970s to the start of the 1990s, an astonishing number of scientists and technicians who were employed by a certain, powerful company died in ways that were deemed by the U.K.'s media – and some notable figures in government too – to be deeply suspicious. Some of those who lost their lives worked on U.S. President Ronald Reagan's Strategic Defense Initiative program – or "Star Wars," as it was famously nicknamed. As for that company, it was the Marconi Electronic Systems, but which, today, exists as a part of BAE Systems Electronics Limited. Its work includes the development of futuristic weaponry and spy-satellite technology.

Of the many who were found dead under dubious and disturbing ways, one was Jonathan Wash. At the time of his death, Wash was working for British Telecom – which had deep connections to Marconi. In 1985, Wash died after falling, or having been pushed, from a window in a hotel room in Ivory Coast, West Africa. It's notable that Wash had suspicions leading up to his death that he was being spied on: watched and followed in a clandestine way. He shared his concerns with his family and friends, but it was all too late. Notably, the British Telecom facility where Wash worked was a top-secret research facility at Martlesham Heath, Suffolk. There is a reason why I make mention of Wash's place of employment, as you'll see now.

A CLOSE-KNIT ENVIRONMENT OF SECRETS

Geographically speaking, let me put all of the above into a shocking perspective for you: the distance from Martlesham Heath to Rendlesham Forest is only 11.3 miles. The journey from Shingle Street to the forest is, at its shortest, only 7.6 miles. A trip from those woods to Bawdsey amounts to less than ten miles. How far might Orford Ness be from Rendlesham Forest? Just 6.8 miles.

A HOTBED OF CONSPIRACIES

All of this tells us something most important. Against a pleasant veneer of old villages, inviting hamlets, ancient woods, and the atmospheric Orford Castle – which was built in the 12th century and still stands tall to this day – the entire area surrounding Rendlesham Forest has, for decades, been an absolute melting pot for top secret activity of the U.K. government. Conspiracies, classified radar-based operations, top secret weapons-development programs, claims of Nazis fried to the bone, and maybe even state-sponsored murder for multiple Marconi scientists and technicians are all parts of the story. *None* of it, however, had a link to UFOs.

As we end this chapter I will leave you with a thought-provoking question: with just about the entire area having been secretly used by the government and the military for decades, then why shouldn't that very same area have been chosen for what happened in Rendlesham Forest in December 1980? I say this location *was* chosen and *was* used –in reckless ways. As has been demonstrated, the higher echelons of U.K. officialdom have skillfully maneuvered their secret ways around the Suffolk landscape very well - and for more than eighty years.

3

'THE IDEA OF APPLYING LASER BEAMS"

To understand how the Rendlesham experiments came into existence, and how the technology involved came to its ultimate fruition, we have to go back to the summer of 1947. It was on June 24 of that year when a pilot named Kenneth Arnold had an astounding encounter with a squadron of strange-looking aircraft near Mt. Rainier, Washington State, USA. Arnold told the eager media the vehicles he saw soared across the skies in a style similar to how a saucer, when thrown, might skip across a body of water. The Flying Saucer – both the name and the phenomenon itself – quickly took a vise-like grip on the imagination of the public. Rather ironically, what Arnold saw were actually delta-shaped craft, and *not* classic saucer-shaped objects. The fact that Arnold didn't really see circular machines was quickly forgotten, though, and people all across the planet soon became familiar with this new mystery in their skies. And with its memorable moniker, too.

As the mystery developed, the U.S. military and the FBI got involved in the investigation of the phenomenon. And when the CIA was created in September 1947, its staff too got into it all. By the latter part of the 1940s just about everyone in the intelligence world was hell-bent on getting the answers to what was flying above their heads. The FBI's primary concerns circled around the possibility that "Communist sympathizers" – maybe even Soviet spies, too - were fabricating some of the tales of Flying Saucers. The purpose being to try and provoke "hysteria" all across the nation. FBI director, J. Edgar Hoover, mused and seethed on the possibility that a top secret arm of the U.S. military itself was possibly secretly building the strange craft as weapons of war – and deliberately keeping Hoover and his agents out of the loop. No wonder he fumed. The military wondered if the Saucers were high-tech devices of Russia. Aliens and distant worlds were on the minds of captains, colonels and generals in the heart of the Pentagon. Fear and paranoia ran rampant within government. It was a crazy unpredictable time.

Certainly, the most visible of all the investigations into the Flying Saucer phenomenon were those undertaken by the U.S. Air Force. Between 1948 and 1969, the Air Force ran three programs to investigate UFOs. They were *Project Sign*, *Project Grudge* and *Project Blue Book*. The conclusion of all three operations was that no evidence was ever found to suggest aliens had visited Earth. Today, numerous UFO researchers conclude that the Air Force's findings were a complete whitewash; an attempt to demystify the mystery, once and for all. There is, however, one particular sidebar of the Air Force's investigations into the UFO phenomenon that has been overlooked by many UFO investigators – and it gets right to the heart of the phenomenon that is the Rendlesham puzzle.

GREAT BALLS OF FIRE!

It's a little known fact that when the Air Force began its UFO investigations in the late 1940s, it quietly farmed out some of the work to companies that had pre-existing, working relationships with the military. As the now-declassified files of *Project Grudge* show, one program in particular was handed over to the Weather Bureau. The Air Force wanted the bureau's staff to find out all that it could on a mysterious, rare, weather-based phenomenon. It is known as ball lightning.

As for what, exactly, ball lightning is, there's this from the *EarthSky* website: "The orbs are typically about the size of a grapefruit, moving slowly over the ground. They have been seen during electrical storms, hence the early theories that they were simply a different form of lightning. They usually disappear after 10 seconds, quietly, but sometimes a bang sound can be heard. They have even been observed to pass through closed windows!"

Martin A. Uman, the chair of the Department of Electrical Computer Engineering in the University of Florida offers these words: "Ball lightning is a well-documented phenomenon in the sense that it has been seen and consistently described by people in all walks of life since the time of the ancient Greeks. There is no accepted theory for what causes it. It does not necessarily consist of plasma; for example, ball lightning could be the result of a chemiluminescent process. The literature abounds with speculations on the physics of the ball lightning."

If you bring up the matter of ball lightning with most UFO researchers, they will likely roll their eyes and dismiss the whole thing with a swift wave of a hand or two. The possibility that some UFO sightings might actually be the result of encounters with nothing weirder than ball lightning causes Flying Saucer seekers to fume, rage and stomp around. And blood-pressure quickly reaches dangerous levels. Believe me, I've seen it all. And it's not a pretty sight.

A STRANGE, NATURAL PHENOMENON

A 1949 *Project Grudge* document contains the results of the Weather Bureau's investigation into ball lightning. The bureau recorded that the mystifying phenomenon was "spherical, roughly globular, egg-shaped, or pear-shaped; many times with projecting streamers; or flame-like irregular 'masses of light.' Luminous in appearance, described in individual cases by different colours but mostly reported as deep red and often as glaring white."

Bureau staff continued: "Some of the cases of 'ball lightning' observed have displayed excrescences of the appearance of little flames emanating from the main body of the luminous mass, or luminous streamers have developed from it and propagated slant-wise toward the ground. In rare instances, it has been reported that the luminous body may break up into a number of smaller balls which may appear to fall towards the earth like a rain of sparks. It has even been reported that the ball has suddenly ejected a whole bundle of many luminous, radiating streamers toward the earth, and then disappeared. There have been reports by observers of 'ball lightning' to the effect that the phenomenon appeared to float through a room or other space for a brief interval of time without making contact with or being attracted by objects."

It all gets really intriguing: the Air Force wasn't overly interested in the possibility that some UFO encounters might have been caused by sightings of ball lightning. What the Air Force *really* wanted were answers to the following intriguing questions: could ball lightning be harnessed and controlled? And better still from the perspective of the military: could the phenomenon itself be weaponized? The answer to both questions was "Yes."

NAZIS IN NEW MEXICO AND TOP SECRET PROGRAMS

In digging into this issue of plans to try and turn ball lightning into a weapon, I discovered that the U.S. Air Force, in 1950, had shared with the U.S. Army certain research it had undertaken at the Maryland-based Edgewood Arsenal. *Fortwiki* provides the following history on the Edgewood Arsenal: "A chemical weapons arsenal established in 1917 and located in the present day Edgewood area of the Aberdeen Proving Ground. The Edgewood area is about 13,000 acres on the west side of the Bush River that was used for the development and testing of chemical agent munitions. This area was originally a separate U.S. Army installation known as Edgewood Arsenal until October 1971 when it merged with Aberdeen Proving Ground and became the Edgewood Area of Aberdeen Proving Ground."

Of the many relevant papers I found at the National Archives, one in particular stood out. It was a letter from the Air Force to Edgewood, and dated May 18, 1950 said: "You are aware we have already discussed with Mr. Clapp the theoretical incendiary applications of ball lightning that might be useful to the several German projects at Kirtland. Useful data should be routed to Mr. Clapp through this office."

While I was unfortunately unable to identify who, exactly, Clapp was, the very fact that he was titled as a "Mr." – rather than as a captain or a colonel and so on - suggests he was not in the direct employ of the military. He may very well have been a scientist, contracted to work on those aforementioned "incendiary applications of ball lightning." As for "Kirtland," that can only be a reference to Kirtland Air Force Base. To this day it is still situated in Albuquerque, New Mexico. On the matter of those "several German projects" housed at Kirtland, there's no doubt at all that this is a direct nod in the direction of *Operation Paperclip*.

It was a program that, in the post-Second World War era, saw hundreds of German scientists (some of who were outright Nazis) secretly brought to New Mexico to continue their dirty work in the field of rocketry. A true Faustian pact? For sure; there is no other way to describe it. What this tells us is that by the start of the 1950s, work was going ahead in the field of ball lightning and its potential uses for the military. And it was going ahead in deep secrecy, too.

THE BIRTH OF THE "KUGELBLITZ"

As my research progressed, I used the Freedom of Information Act and requested – from many of the ABC agencies within government - copies of any and all papers dealing with ball lightning. Some of the material released to me was highly intriguing. The long list included: *Theory of the Lightning Ball and its Application to the Atmospheric Phenomenon Called 'Flying Saucers'*, put together by Carl Benadicks in 1954; *Ball Lightning: A Survey*, prepared by one J.R. McNally for the Oak Ridge National Laboratory, Tennessee [year unknown]; D.V. Ritchie's *Reds May Use Lightning as a Weapon*, which popped up in the pages of *Missiles and Rockets* in August 1959; and *An Experimental and Theoretical Program to Investigate the Feasibility of Confining Plasma in Free Space by Radar Beams*, the latter being the work of a C.M. Haaland, in 1960, for the Armor Research Foundation, situated in the Illinois Institute of Technology.

One document really stood out: *Survey of Kugelblitz Theories for Electromagnetic Incendiaries*. It was the brainchild of W.B. Lyttle and C.E. Wilson. At the time, they were in the employ of Melpar, Inc., which is described as "an American government contractor in the 20th century Cold War period. At a time when most employment in Washington, D.C. was directly by the U.S. federal government,

Melpar became an early private sector contracting company training a high technology workforce in the area."

As for the word "Kugelblitz," it's German for ball lightning.

HOW TO WEAPONIZE NATURAL PHENOMENA

Lyttle and Wilson were assigned to the Edgewood Arsenal, and to what was intriguingly titled as a "New Concepts Division / Special Projects" operation. At the beginning of their 92-pages-long report, the two wrote: "The purpose of this study was to review the theory and *experimental data on ball lightning*, to compare the existing theory and experimental data to determine whether ball lightning is a high or low energy phenomenon, and if it is a high energy phenomenon define an effective theoretical and experimental program *to develop a potential incendiary weapon* [italics mine]."

They added: "Three major categories were established for the purpose of grouping the numerous theories on the subject. These categories are the classical plasma theories, the quantum plasma theories, and the non-plasma theories. A theoretical and experimental Kugelblitz program is recommended by which the most promising high energy theories could be developed so that a weapons application could be realized."

On the matter of what, exactly, ball lightning was, the pair had a few ideas. Those same ideas included a "plasma created by a lightning strike and maintained by electromagnetic standing waves;" a "non-plasma phenomenon;" and the "nuclear theory;" which was "based on the assumption that the content of the ball is radioactive carbon-14 created from atmospheric nitrogen by the action of thermal neutrons liberated by a lightning strike." Wilson and Lyttle said, "since the high energy Kugelblitz is clearly the only type weapon of importance, we believe that the major effort should be expended along these lines."

As the work progressed, matters got more and more energized. The two men reported: "If Kugelblitz is to be developed as a distinctive weapon, a means of guiding the energy concentration toward a potential target must be achieved. Some preliminary considerations on this subject have resulted in the idea of applying laser beams to such a task."

The pair explained that the "modulation of the vertical component of [a] laser incident" would allow for the "control of the Kugelblitz." They added that the "forces necessary for guidance only will depend on local charges, as well as the net Kugelblitz charge and wind forces. The problem is a difficult one, but some light is beginning to appear on the subject. A concentrated analytical and experimental effort should be made soon as the implications of successful work could be far reaching. Only an adequately planned programme, utilizing a full time, competent staff with adequate equipment, can hope to succeed within a reasonable time period."

You may wonder: how does any of this have a bearing on what occurred in Rendlesham Forest? Let us take a look. You may be shocked by what you are about to see.

"LIKE A RAIN OF SPARKS"

Recall that Lieutenant Colonel Halt prepared and submitted his now-famous memo to the Ministry of Defense around two weeks after the incidents occurred. In part, Halt wrote that a "red sun-like light was seen through the trees. It moved about and pulsed. At one point it appeared to throw off glowing particles and then broke into five separate white objects and then disappeared. Immediately thereafter, three star-like objects were noticed in the sky...the object to the south was visible for two or three hours and beamed down a stream of light from time to time."

Reports of beams of light seen in conjunction with moving lights that ejected bright particles, sound very much like someone putting into practice the theoretical plans cited within the pages of the *Survey of Kugelblitz Theories for Electromagnetic Incendiaries* document. Namely: the control and utilization of ball lightning-style phenomena via lasers. Certainly, Halt's description of the strange phenomena in the woods appearing to "throw off glowing particles" sounds astonishingly like the words that the U.S. Weather Bureau used way back in 1948 to describe ball lightning: "...it has been reported that the luminous body may *break up into a number of smaller balls* which may appear to fall towards the earth *like a rain of sparks*. It has even been reported that the ball has suddenly ejected *a whole bundle of many luminous, radiating streamers toward the earth* [italics all mine]" And, there's Halt's reference to a "red sun-like light." Ball lightning - with its globular form - does indeed resemble something akin to a brightly lit sun. There's more to come.

LASERS, BALL LIGHTNING AND THE
"CONTROL OF THE KUGELBLITZ"

Georgina Bruni, whose book on Rendlesham – *You Can't Tell the People* – makes for essential reading, said: "Halt has always insisted that during the incident a pencil-thin beam hit the ground just a few feet away from where he was positioned."

Halt did indeed say that. In his own words: "The object was coming at us at a very high rate of speed. One of these beams of light fell very, very close to us, sort of a pencil beam of light." Bruni continued and speculated that Rendlesham may have been "an experiment, and the beam was a laser."

With that said, it's time to go back to what Wilson and Lyttle reported in their document: "If Kugelblitz is to be developed as a distinctive weapon, a means of guiding the energy concentration toward a potential target must be achieved. Some preliminary considerations on this subject have resulted in the idea of applying laser beams to such a task." The "*modulation of the vertical component of a laser incident*" would permit for the "*control of the Kugelblitz* [italics mine]."

KUGELBLITZ AND RENDLESHAM PARALLELS

So, we have Lyttle and Wilson discussing how laser beams could be used to guide ball lightning to its target. And we have Colonel Halt stating that a "pencil-thin" laser-like beam was seen in the woods at the very same time the strange aerial phenomena was present. There are clear and obvious parallels between (A) the "rain of sparks" that the Weather Bureau described in relation to ball lightning in the 1960s; and (B) the phenomenon that "appeared to throw off glowing particles" in Rendlesham Forest in 1980. It's tough indeed to deny the astonishing similarities and parallels present here. They are right there in front of us, documented in Colonel Halt's memorandum and in the pages of the Lyttle-Wilson *Survey of Kugelblitz Theories for Electromagnetic Incendiaries.*

The work of Lyttle and Wilson was completed in 1965. That was a long time ago. It was, however, only fifteen years before those fringe-like phenomena appeared in and above a certain English forest. That would have been plenty of time for those on the secret program to perfect the ball lightning-based work - and using lasers - to an even greater and far more sophisticated degree. So, we have plausible explanations for *some* of the primary phenomena seen in those English woods – none of which requires an extraterrestrial component to it.

We are nowhere near done with the high-tech programs that were running at the Edgewood Arsenal. It's time to begin our look at the matter of mind-manipulation; something that may have been secretly applied to some of the men out in the forest.

4

"CLOUDS OF PSYCHOCHEMICALS"

On December 9, 2012, *The New Yorker* ran an article titled "Operation Delirium: Decades after a risky Cold War experiment, a scientist lives with secrets." The scientist was one Colonel James S. Ketchum, who spent approximately two decades in the U.S. Army. Ketchum "became the military's leading expert in a secret Cold War experiment to fight enemies with clouds of psychochemicals that temporarily incapacitate the mind - causing, in the words of one ranking officer, a 'selective malfunctioning of the human machine.'"

It turns out this highly classified program of mind-control was secretly run inside the confines of the Edgewood Arsenal. As we saw in the previous chapter, Edgewood was *the very same place* where secret research into controllable UFO-like ball lightning was studied. It was all achieved in the "New Concepts Division / Special Projects" program.

Journalist Raffi Khatchadourian asked: "Were the human experiments there a Dachau-like horror, or were they sound and necessary science? As veterans of the tests have come forward, their unanswered questions have slowly gathered into a kind of historical undertow, and Ketchum, more than anyone else, has been caught in its pull. In 2006, he self-published a memoir, 'Chemical Warfare: Secrets Almost Forgotten,' which defended the research."

As for the outcome of the lawsuit, the *Washington Post*, in a June 4, 2019 feature ("James Ketchum, who conducted mind-altering experiments on soldiers, dies at 87"), stated: "Dr. Ketchum's archives featured in a 2009 class-action lawsuit, filed by a veterans' advocacy group on behalf of soldiers who participated in the chemical weapons testing program. In 2017, the U.S. District Court for Northern District of California ordered the Army to provide medical care to the surviving volunteers."

"ABOUT 7,000 SOLDIERS TOOK PART IN THESE EXPERIMENTS"

For many of those soldiers, however, it was all too little and all too late. The Department of Veterans Affairs has highlighted the history of the Edgewood experiments in concise-but-to-the-point words:

From 1955 to 1975, the U.S. Army Chemical Corps conducted classified medical studies at Edgewood Arsenal, Maryland [Author's note: the very location where the Kugelblitz program secretly went ahead]. The purpose was to evaluate the impact of low-dose chemical warfare agents on military personnel and to test protective clothing and pharmaceuticals. If you are concerned about exposures during Edgewood/Aberdeen chemical tests, talk to your health care provider or local VA Environmental Health Coordinator.

About 7,000 soldiers took part in these experiments that involved exposures to more than 250 different chemicals, according to the Department of Defense (DoD). Some of the volunteers exhibited certain symptoms at the time of exposure to these agents. Long-term follow-up was not planned as part of the DoD studies.

The National Academies of Science (NAS) reviewed the potential for long-term health effects from these experiments and did not find any significant long-term physical harm, except for some Veterans exposed to larger doses of mustard agents. NAS published these studies under the title of, "Possible Long-Term Health Effects of Short-Term Exposure to Chemical Agents," in three volumes dated 1982, 1984 and 1985.

"SENSATIONS SEEM REAL, BUT THEY ARE CREATED BY THE MIND"

In a 2004 follow-up report, "Health Effects of Perceived Exposure to Biochemical Warfare Agents," NAS concluded that post-traumatic stress disorder (PTSD) could occur as a result of 'perceived exposure to biochemical warfare agents.'" We're told much more about the kind of experimentation that went on at the Edgewood Arsenal:

The Health and Medicine Division (formerly known as the Institute of Medicine) report, *Updated Literature Review of Sarin (2004)*, found that research doesn't show long-term neurological problems from exposure to low levels of sarin. A low level of sarin is an amount that doesn't cause noticeable symptoms during the exposure.

The agents tested included chemical warfare agents and other related agents (inactive substances or placebos such as saline were used):

- Anticholinesterase nerve agents (ex., sarin and common organophosphorus (OP), and carbamate pesticides)
- Mustard agents

- Nerve agent antidotes atropine and scopolamine
- Nerve agent reactivators (ex., the common OP antidote 2-PAM chloride)
- Psychoactive agents (ex., LSD, PCP, cannaboids, and BZ)
- Irritants and riot control agents
- Alcohol and caffeine

There ends the data provided by the U.S. Department of Veterans Affairs, which is most revealing. Of particular interest is the fact LSD and BZ were tested on military volunteers at the Edgewood Arsenal, the home to classified ball lightning experiments. Both have the ability to provoke dazzling imagery in the human mind. Sometimes, depending on the setting and the mood, terrifying visions can occur. Dare I say alien visions? Yes, I dare. And the reason why I dare is because soon we'll see evidence the men in Rendlesham Forest were exposed to certain hallucinogens.

Medscape say: "The chemical warfare agent 3-quinuclidinyl benzilate (QNB, BZ) is an anticholinergic agent that affects both the peripheral and central nervous systems (CNS). It is one of the most potent anticholinergic psychomimetics known, with only small doses necessary to produce incapacitation. It is classified as a hallucinogenic chemical warfare agent. QNB usually is disseminated as an aerosol, and the primary route of absorption is through the respiratory system. Absorption also can occur through the skin or gastrointestinal tract. It is odorless. QNB's pharmacologic activity is similar to other anticholinergic drugs (e.g., atropine) but with a much longer duration of action."

As for LSD, *Medical News Today* says it is a "semi-synthetic drug that combines natural and man-made substances. It is derived from ergot, a fungus that grows on certain grains, and a non-organic chemical called diethylamide. It stimulates serotonin production in the cortex and deep structures of the brain, by activating serotonin receptors. These receptors help visualize and interpret the real world. The additional serotonin allows more stimuli to be processed that usual. Normally, the brain filters out irrelevant stimuli, but with LSD this is not the case. This overstimulation causes changes in thought, attention, perceptions, and emotions. These alterations appear as hallucinations. *Sensations seem real, but they are created by the mind* [italics mine]. The perceptions can involve one or more of the five senses. It can also cause blending of the senses, known as synesthesia. People report 'hearing' colors and 'seeing' sounds."

"TESTS THAT MIGHT HAVE EXPOSED SERVICE MEMBERS"

There is also the matter of a certain *Project 112*. Of this innocuously titled operation, the U.S. Government Accountability Office says: "In the 1962-74 time period, the Department of Defense (DOD) conducted a classified chemical and biological warfare test program *Project 112* that might have exposed service members and civilian personnel to chemical or biological agents. In 2000 the Department of Veterans Affairs (VA) began obtaining information from DOD about the program. Concerned that veterans and others might have health problems from exposure during *Project 112* and similar DOD tests, Congress required DOD in the 2003 Defense Authorization Act to identify Project 112 tests and personnel potentially exposed service members and the number of civilian personnel and other chemical and biological tests that might have exposed service members. GAO was required by the act and subsequent guidance from the congressional requesters to evaluate (1) DOD's process to identify the *Project 112* tests and the service members and the number of civilian personnel potentially exposed, (2) DOD's progress in identifying similar tests outside *Project 112*."

The study demonstrated that, yet again, volunteers had suffered adversely from exposure to hallucinogens. It's very important to note that although *Project 112* was a U.S. program, personnel from the U.K.'s chemical and biological research facility at Porton Down, Wiltshire, England, were also very much connected to the studies. And, as you will soon see, Porton Down is at the absolute core of the incidents that occurred in Rendlesham Forest in 1980. The picture – bit-by-bit, and strand-by-strand – is coming together. It goes without saying that LSD, 3-quinuclidinyl benzilate, laser-guided ball lightning, a "New Concepts Division," and *Project 112* – and *each and every one of them* secretly and directly connected to the Edgewood Arsenal - make for a distinctly heady cocktail of head-spinning proportions.

Let us now see how Porton Down's scientists became implicated in this ever-expanding story. And, also of how and why Georgina Bruni decided to go searching for the truth behind the Rendlesham Forest-Porton Down connection.

5

"ONE THOUGHT HE WAS
SEEING TIGERS"

In view of what we learned in the previous chapter, we now have to take a closer look at the work and the history of Porton Down and why and how it played such a key role in the Rendlesham Forest situation. Here's what I wrote in Dr. Robert M. Wood's book, *Alien Viruses*:

"Although work at Porton Down had originally begun in March 1916, it was not until 1940 that the installation became the central hub of British interest in biological warfare. Following the start of the Second World War, a highly secret and independent group – the Biology Department, Porton - was established by the War Cabinet, with a mandate to investigate the reality of biological warfare and to develop a means of retaliation in the event that biological warfare was utilized against the United Kingdom. By 1946, the name of the wartime group had become the Microbiological Research Department. A decade later, the biological warfare research of Porton Down's staff had become solely defensive in nature; and in 1957 it was re-named the Microbiological Research Establishment.

"By the 1970s it was decided that the MRE should be placed under the aegis of a civil authority, and on 1 April 1979, it became known as the Center for Applied Microbiology and Research. In 1995, the Establishment became part of the Defense Evaluation and Research Agency, and six years later DERA split into two organizations: QinetiQ, a private company, and the Defense Science and Technology Laboratory) which remains an agency of the Ministry of Defense. Today, Porton Down is known by its two facilities: Defense Science and Technology Laboratory (DSTL), Porton Down, and Public Health England (PHE)."

"VERY FEW SERVICEMEN KNEW WHAT THEY WERE VOLUNTEERING FOR"

As the BBC note, U.K. military personnel were regularly used in secret mind-altering experiments at Porton Down in the 1950s and 1960s. So, why not use American personnel who were stationed to the United Kingdom in December 1980? Keep that question in mind, as it will resurface soon. The BBC says: "Porton Down was set up in 1916. It was a center designed to test chemical and biological weapons. Nerve gases such as Sarin and CS gas were tested on volunteer servicemen. Servicemen were offered around £2 and three days leave as an incentive to take part in tests. Very few servicemen knew what they were volunteering for and some were even told it was research into the cure for the common cold. In 1953 it is alleged that serviceman Ronald Maddison died after taking part in a Sarin gas experiment. In 1962, one of Porton Down's own scientists, Geoffrey Bacon died of the plague. Since the end of WWII, 20,000 people have taken part in experiments at Porton Down."

LSD was tested at Porton Down, too. On military personnel, no less. And as the *Guardian* newspaper stated in 2005: "Fifty years ago, Eric Gow had a baffling and unexplained experience. As a 19-year-old sailor, he remembers going to a clandestine military establishment, where he was given something to drink in a sherry glass and experienced vivid hallucinations. Other servicemen also remember tripping: one thought he was seeing tigers jumping out of a wall, while another recalls faces 'with eyes running down their cheeks, Salvador Dalí-style.' Mr. Gow and another serviceman had volunteered to take part in what they thought was research to find a cure for the common cold. Mr. Gow felt the government had never explained what happened to him. But now he has received an official admission for the first time, confirmed last night, the intelligence agency MI6 tested LSD on servicemen."

FROM PORTON DOWN TO RENDLESHAM FOREST

Let us now address the back-story concerning how Georgina Bruni and I came to conclude there was an undeniable connection between Porton Down and certain matters that happened in Rendlesham Forest in 1980. I first met Georgina in 1997. It was in London, at an evening party held by my then-literary-agent, Andrew Lownie. Andrew got me deals for three books with Simon & Schuster. They were *A Covert Agenda*; *The FBI Files*; and *Cosmic Crashes*. At the time, Georgina was already working on her Rendlesham book, *You Can't Tell the People*. It was published in November 2000. Georgina and I hung out at Andrew's party and, as a result, a friendship was forged. That friendship continued until Georgina's death in 2008.

Back in the late 1990s, Georgina and I were two of a very small cadre of people in the U.K.-based UFO community who were actively and regularly investigating the UFO-Porton Down links. As a result of this, we agreed to quietly and carefully share our data – including any and all new data as it came along – with each other. And that's how I came to become a recipient of Georgina's astonishing information on the Rendlesham story.

As the research for her book advanced, Georgina discovered that in late December 1980 a team from Porton Down was dispatched into the heart of Rendlesham Forest. Dressed in full-body protection (hazmat) outfits, they entered into the woods on a classified operation. It was assumed among those in the UFO research community who Georgina had confided in, that the Porton Down team was there to try and determine what happened over the course of those three nights and to see if there were any chemical or biological hazards still present. Georgina assumed that, and so did I. *At the time*, at least. The truth turned out to be much different, however.

Georgina confided in me a list of various characters in this story who knew of the Porton Down ties to Rendlesham. By "a list" I mean she gave me the names of several people who had confided in her. Georgina was clearly worried about what she had uncovered – to the extent that she asked me to sign a sheet of paper that basically stated I would not reveal the names of those sources. It certainly wasn't a legally-bounding contract, but, out of respect for Georgina, I agreed to take it as exactly that. I'm sure part of the reason was because Georgina wanted to get the scoop on the case for her own book – which, as an author myself, is something I can easily understand. That said, I also got a feeling Georgina had certain concerns about publicizing the names of the people who were sitting on the Porton Down story – and who had done so for years. So, with the names hidden, all was good between me and Georgina.

As for Georgina's sources and their claims, the following is what I know for sure, today: one of them is dead and his family claim to have no knowledge of the story concerning Rendlesham Forest. The family has, however, grudgingly admitted the relative in question *did* indeed work at Porton Down: from 1978 until 1986. Two of the informants have fairly rare surnames, something that made it relatively easy for me to find them. Of those two, one consistently failed to reply to my letters and phone-messages. The other was a Scotsman. Now long-retired from the Royal Air Force Police, he told me in three succinct, amusing and memorable words: "fuck off, laddie."

Such were Georgina's concerns about sharing this part of the Porton Down story, she refused to email the information and names to me. Instead, she sent everything by regular mail.

PORTON DOWN GETS BUSY

Georgina's book presents the theory that the Porton Down team arrived at Rendlesham Forest on the morning *after* the first night. And they were there to try and assess what had happened, when UFOs appeared, on the night *before*. As Georgina learned shortly after her book was published, however (something that, admittedly, was just about the most unfortunate timing possible), the Porton Down team actually arrived one night *before* the first "encounter" in the woods, and *not* shortly after the initial incident, as has been assumed for so long.

The reality of the situation is that the group from Porton Down were there to carefully, and ruthlessly, help set the grim scene for what was planned to go down on the famous, first night in December. The terrible truth is the team from Porton Down *wasn't* there to investigate presumed UFO incidents at all: *they were there to secretly help create them*. There were rumors – Georgina heard - the plan involved, on the first night, the quiet and careful release of what Georgina described as "low-grade" aerosol-based hallucinogens in the woods, courtesy of Porton Down's scientists. Time-wise, this was planned to take place in precise conjunction with those who were handling the ball lightning and the aerial display. It was a display that would soon engulf the Air Force personnel who were caught up in the swirling maelstrom in the trees.

You don't have to rely on my words in relation to these Porton Down-based claims. The author of a very-well-received, non-fiction book on biological- and chemical-warfare, and whose work was also focused heavily on the history surrounding top secret brain-screwing at Porton Down, knew a great deal of this, too. I emailed that same author on many occasions. I didn't get even a single reply. The last time I emailed her was April 2, 2020. Not a word. Silence speaks volumes, as they say. And, as Nick Pope noted in his book with John Burroughs and Jim Pennistion, *Encounter in Rendlesham Forest*, there were certain figures who knew of the Porton Down angle and who "had strong links with the MoD."

6

"UFO INCIDENTS THAT HAVE SIGNIFICANT DATES"

As we know, the primary events occurred on the night of December 26, 1980 – and well into the early hours. Bringing in a team from Porton Down on the evening before it all began – to ensure things were ready to go – would have made a great deal of sense. And here is why: The day before the Rendlesham incidents began was Christmas Day: December 25. This particular holiday period is very much a grand ritual in the U.K. – and probably even more so back then than today. Christmas Day in the U.K. usually goes like this: we open our gifts and presents in the morning, have a large turkey lunch in the afternoon, watch the tedious "Queen's Speech" that Elizabeth II delivers to the nation every year, and then sit back and watch whatever blockbuster movies have been chosen to entertain us all. Back then, it was all but guaranteed it would be a *James Bond* movie. See what I mean about rituals? So, where is this all going? I'll tell you.

In the U.K., Christmas Day is the *one* day of the year when almost everyone – the emergency services and other vital bodies excluded – are celebrating Christmas at home. We're talking about tens of millions of people all indoors, but who for the rest of the year would be going about their daily business. The roads are quiet on Christmas Day. The sidewalks are largely deserted. Back then, also, most of the nation's stores were closed on Christmas Day. The pubs were shut, too. Restaurants were closed for business. Cinemas weren't open. Get the picture? Most people, then, were in their homes – and they stayed that way for the whole of that day. Most important of all, that would have been exactly the same for the people who lived near to Rendlesham Forest and its surroundings: they would likely have been at home, too, tucking into tasty meals, having a few drinks or more, celebrating the holidays, and then crashing out for a few hours after that mountain of food and plenty of booze.

What all of this tells us is that Christmas Day – albeit probably in the late evening hours – would have been the ideal time to have begun the first stage of the experiment. That is, making sure the Porton Down team had plenty of time to confirm that those low-grade hallucinogens were in place and primed to be deployed on the next night. And without any interference from the local public, who were way too busy with Christmas.

All of this demonstrates that very few people in the area would have been on the roads on that day of all days – and on that night, too. Here's an important observation: even the base personnel themselves, we know for sure, were on a skeleton-staff as Christmas Day came around. Many of them, too, celebrated with their friends and families. That was a significant part of the dark plot. It wasn't just the public who were oblivious to what was happening; it was also more than a few military people who were stationed in the Woodbridge-Bentwaters area. Less numbers of people around meant less chances of the plan becoming compromised. The next night turned out to be perfect timing, too.

AND YET ANOTHER WAY TO KEEP A TOP-SECRET PROGRAM OUT OF VIEW

In the U.K., December 26 is also a longstanding holiday for the majority of the populace. It's called Boxing Day. Writer Christopher Klein says: "December 26 is not only a day for Santa Claus to catch his breath but a public holiday known as Boxing Day in the United Kingdom and other British Commonwealth countries such as Australia, Canada and New Zealand. In spite of its peculiar name, Boxing Day has nothing to do with fisticuffs, the trashing of empty boxes left over from Christmas or the return of unwanted presents to department stores. The term is of British origin, and the Oxford English Dictionary traces its earliest print attribution to 1833, four years before Charles Dickens referred to it in 'The Pickwick Papers.'"

Elaine Lemm explains its history. She says: "A 'Christmas Box' in Britain is a name for a Christmas present. Boxing Day was traditionally a day off for servants and the day when they received a 'Christmas Box' from the master. The servants would also go home on Boxing Day to give 'Christmas Boxes' to their families." Lemm describes another theory on the origin and name of this one-day-long holiday: "A box to collect money for the poor traditionally and placed in Churches on Christmas day and opened the next day - which is Boxing Day."

Other theories exist for this old tradition, but those are certainly the primary ones. So, not only do we have most people at home on Christmas Day, but on Boxing Day, too. Three days and nights of experiments, and three days and nights of the people living near to Rendlesham Forest and doing not a great deal at all. The specific timing of Porton Down's part of the experiment was, I strongly suspect, chosen deliberately and could not have been better.

THE IMPORTANCE OF DATES

It's time to make a brief diversion. Of sorts. But, still in relation to the importance of dates. Since the early 1980s, reports have surfaced all over the world of a type of UFO that has become known as the "Black Triangle." They look not unlike the Lockheed F-117 *Nighthawk* (more popularly referred to as the Stealth Fighter) and the Northrop B-2 *Spirit* (better known as the Stealth Bomber), but are much larger and have the capability to fly almost silently. While there have been more than a few interesting eyewitness reports, there are two cases that really stand out. One was a wave of craft seen above Belgium and that reached its peak at the end of March 1990. The other was of a single craft flying across the skies of the U.K., in 1993 – and *also* at the end of March. In both cases and countries, there were multiple witnesses, some of whom were military personnel and police officers.

Nick Pope, while still in the employ of the Ministry of Defense, at the time was involved in the investigations of the 1993 event in the U.K. And, as a result of his quest to find the truth, he proactively chose to liaise with military personnel in Belgium. I interviewed Pope extensively about the sightings of the Flying Triangles – in both nations – and how the Ministry of Defense had handled things. Pope said to me that while he was addressing the U.K.-based sightings, "one interesting point occurred." He explained what he meant: "We were dealing with activity, on exactly the same night in March, but three years later." Pope added it was very similar to the "very famous wave of sightings of very similar craft seen over Belgium. And my favorite theory about this - or at least an idea I floated about - was that this was a deliberate move on the part of whoever was operating the craft."

Pope explained his thoughts on this to me: "If the media had got a hold of this, it would have been too late to get it in the newspapers on March 31. So, the earliest date that the story could have run here, in the U.K., would have been April 1 – April Fools' Day. The same for the Belgium wave: March 31 and [into] April Fools' Day. A little indicator, perhaps, of an intelligence and possibly even some form of humor."

I have to say, I completely reject the idea aliens have even the slightest awareness of what goes on during April 1; it's just about the wackiest and lamest thing I've heard in a very long time. Christmas Day and Boxing Day were carefully, and deliberately, chosen for a particular reason in relation to the Rendlesham Forest case: to ensure there would be a minimum of people around when the experiments really got going. April Fools' Day, I suggest, was an important factor in what happened in 1990 and 1993. The goal? To ensure that if the media got onto the stories, and published them on the earliest date possible – which would have been April 1 - the headlines would have been all about little green men, and *not* about far more serious and sensitive issues, such as secret night-flights of highly-classified, futuristic aircraft of someone's military.

Perhaps, someone reading this book may decide to look at *other*, fantastic UFO incidents that have significant dates attached to them. Possibly, a fascinating and rarely-considered trend that has been overlooked for so long will soon become much clearer – and, in the process, shown to have been very effective when it came to matters relative to military operations and strange deceptions involving non-existent aliens.

MAKING THE STORY EVEN STRANGER

There may be another aspect of the Rendlesham Forest legend that prompted the people behind the experiments to choose that particular area of woods for their tests. Rendlesham Forest has a long history of ghostly encounters. Witchcraft and occult-based rites and rituals have been performed late at night in those dark woods. So-called "Alien Big Cats," or "black panthers," as they are mostly named, have been seen roaming through the woods on more than a few times. One of the earliest, credible cases on record is that of Jimmy Freeman, whose close encounter with a big cat occurred while driving past Rendlesham Forest late one night in the mid-1970s. While the precise date has been lost to the inevitable fog of time, the details are as fresh in the mind of Freeman today as they were on the night the incident occurred.

Given the fact that the encounter had occurred around 11:15 to 11:30 on what was a dark, cloudy and slightly misty night, Freeman was driving slowly and had his lights on full-beam as he negotiated the dark and winding roads. As a result, when something large and shadowy charged across the road in front of him, Freeman could not fail to see the creature for what it was. Long, sleek and black in color, Freeman is in no doubt that for a split second or two he had a brief sighting of a huge cat. Today, he says firmly: "If I live to be a hundred, I will tell the same: Rendlesham Forest has big cats."

On a cold winter's afternoon in 1983, the then-soon-to-be-married Paul and Jane Jennings were blissfully strolling through those woods when they were terrified by the sudden manifestation in front of them of what Jane would describe succinctly as "a big black dog." She elaborated that the pair had been walking along a pathway when, on rounding a bend, they came face to face with the phantom beast – something that prompted Jane to intriguingly add: "It was almost like it was waiting for us." Far more shocking, however, was what happened next. Suddenly, the beast began to flicker on and off for four or five times, then finally vanished, literally, before the Jennings' eyes amid an overwhelming smell that reminded the pair of burning metal. Not surprisingly, the terrified couple fled for the safety of their car and fled the area. The U.K.'s "phantom black dogs," as they are popularly known, prompted none other than Sir Arthur Conan Doyle – the creator of Sherlock Holmes – to write his classic novel, *The Hound of the Baskervilles*.

Rendlesham Forest, as well as the Suffolk locales of West Wratting and Balsham, is reportedly home to an even more dia- bolical beast than the phantom black dog. It is a creature that has come to be known locally as the Shug-Monkey. Described as being a bizarre combination of giant dog and large ape, the creature is said to strike deep terror into the hearts of those souls unfortunate enough to cross its path. And you thought that UFOs were the strangest things to be found in Rendlesham Forest, right? Wrong. It's a magnet for strange phenomena – and it has been for a long, long time. It is, however, Rendlesham Forest's UFO connection that has made those woods world-famous.

In many respects, it doesn't really matter if you are a believer or a disbeliever in supernatural phenomena, such as large and mysterious cats, ghostly hounds and a weird ape-like beast. The important thing to note is this: Rendlesham Forest has a reputation of being distinctly creepy for reasons that go far beyond UFOs and aliens, as you have just seen. If you wanted to run a secret project in an area of English woodland, then what better place could there be than Rendlesham Forest? The answer is simple: there *is* no better location. Here's why: Those who *do* believe in the paranormal will likely say that tales of mysterious creatures seen in the woods *only serve to reinforce* the idea aliens landed at Rendlesham – which is almost certainly what the people who concocted the experiments were counting on.

After all, the renowned expert on all-things supernatural, John Keel – noted most of all for his 1975 book, *The Mothman Prophecies* - came to believe that Bigfoot, UFOs, aliens, the Djinn, the Loch Ness Monster and more mysterious entities were all inter-connected. Using an area of woods – for nefarious reasons - that *already* had a reputation for being drenched in unearthly phenomena, would amount to perfect planning. When the "UFOs" put in their appearances at Christmas 1980, it was just another addition to the *already-bulging* collection of tales of the unknown that came from within Rendlesham Forest. And, because of the eerie reputation that the woods had (and still have), no one was thinking about secret experiments of government agencies.

7

"IN REALITY THE 'VOLUNTEERS' WERE ALL DUPES"

Back to Georgina Bruni: her final source told a most sinister tale. It concerns a military base situated in the county of Norfolk, England. It borders the county of Suffolk, where the Rendlesham events happened. Royal Air Force Watton is a now-closed-down RAF facility that opened in 1939. The *History of Watton* website provides the following on the base: "The station was opened on the 4th January 1939 under the command of Group Captain F.J. Vincent as a station of 2 Group, Bomber Command. It was built as part of the R.A.F. expansion program of 1935 / 1936 on farmland that was well known locally as good mushroom land and under the right conditions mushrooms are still to be seen in quantity in the area."

Although a part of me *really* wants to expand on the mushrooms angle, I don't think there is a connection – even though I dearly wish there was!

Bringing matters up to latter day times, *History of Watton* also notes: "The decision to dispose of RAF Watton was a long time in coming mainly because of political ineptitude. All maintenance of the buildings ceased in 1994 and the site was let to go. It wasn't until 1998 that the Station was sold, by which time it was in a very run-down state. The Airfield remained and still remains in the hands of the Ministry of Defense."

Now to the story as told to Georgina Bruni.

RADAR RECORDS AND HAZMAT OUTFITS

On October 25, 1988, Squadron Leader E.E. Webster of RAF Watton wrote me the following after I raised questions about RAF Watton's claimed connections to the Rendlesham Forest case: "Our log book for the period does indeed say that a UFO was reported to us by RAF Bentwaters at 0325 GMT on 28 December 1980 but that is all the information we have."

Apparently, though, it actually *wasn't* "all the information we have." Someone – or an agency - was being decidedly economic with the facts, such as those facts were. Nick Pope revealed that Georgina Bruni's RAF Police sources knew of a far greater story concerning RAF Watton than the brief one provided to me by Squadron Leader E.E. Webster in 1988. Apparently, on the very same night that staff at RAF Watton recorded the presence of a UFO (on December 28, 1980), a pair of military dog-handlers were patrolling the facility when something very strange happened.

The pair was shocked and baffled to see just outside the perimeter fence a number of figures. No, they were not aliens. They were all too human: they were dressed in NBC (Nuclear, Biological and Chemical) outfits, head-to-foot. One of Bruni's police sources revealed he and his comrades were interviewed, questioned, and warned to remain silent with regard to what they had seen on that cold, winter's night. Or, rather, *who* they had seen. Their police notebooks were taken from them, as were what Nick Pope describes as "various logbooks."

It all smacked of a cover-up. Those with an interest in what happened in Rendlesham Forest weren't going to let matters go by, however. No way. We will return to RAF Watton later – and in a very strange way that expands further on the matter of UFOs and radar.

"NO RECORDS" WHAT DID WE EXPECT?

It was in January 2001 that the then-retired - and now late - British Admiral of the Fleet, Lord Hill-Norton, decided to get into the Rendlesham Forest controversy. Having had an interest in UFOs for decades, he used his considerable clout to try and figure out what occurred in 1980. It was hardly an easy task for Hill-Norton to achieve. Of specific interest to Hill-Norton were the claims of a connection to the activities of the Porton Down staff. He wanted to know "whether personnel from Porton Down visited Rendlesham Forest or the area surrounding RAF Watton in December 1980 or January 1981; and whether they are aware of any tests carried out in either of those two areas aimed at assessing any nuclear, biological or chemical hazard."

Hill-Norton got a response from the government he had dutifully worked for. It was not, however, the reply he hoped for. The reply came from Baroness Symons of Vernham Dean. She spoke on behalf of the MoD, who provided nothing but a concise comment that didn't really advance the investigation into the case at all. The baroness said: "The staff at the Defense Evaluation and Research Agency (DERA) Chemic and Biological Defense (CBD) laboratories at Porton Down have made a thorough search of their archives and have found no record of any such visits."

It has to be said that government agencies – and their fawning lackeys – can be extremely careful about what they say and how they say it. It should be noted that Baroness Symons never said that there was no Rendlesham-Porton link. What she said was that no evidence of such a connection had been found. That's a very different thing, altogether. Playing things carefully and tactfully provides government personnel with a perfect "get out clause," in the event that additional information might later surface that shows the earlier claims to have been erroneous.

"THE 'VOLUNTEERS' WERE ALL DUPES"

Still keeping a careful eye on Porton Down: as I postulate, the Rendlesham case was not a UFO incident. In terms of getting the answers, we should be looking at (A) the Kugelblitz experiments of decades ago; (B) that intriguing Porton Down presence in the woods in December 1980; and (C) mind-altering technology tested under the banner of a staged alien event. If you're serving in the military and under the influence of something that can have you seeing "tigers jumping out of a wall," then maybe seeing something akin to an extraterrestrial creature may not be as strange as it might seem to be. If all of this stretches your imagination just too far, I refer you to the next part of the story.

What Georgina Bruni presented as a possibility, and that I accept as a downright reality, isn't just feasible: it's completely plausible. Something very similar was secretly undertaken *sixteen years before* anyone was talking about aliens in Rendlesham Forest. Drugs, woods, hallucinogens and military personnel having their brains blasted into orbit: they were all parts of something that happened way back in 1964 – and very near to Porton Down.

SMALL CHANGE, MONEYBAGS AND RECOUNT:
SECRET PROGRAMS AND LSD IN THE WOODS

Porton Down's almost obsessive interest in experimentation involving hallucinogens, and particularly so LSD, dates back to the early years of the 1950s – although, incredibly, this was completely hidden from the people of the U.K. until the early years of the 21st century. Such is the nature of what passes for "Freedom of Information" in the U.K. As the 1950s progressed, however, more and more research was undertaken – on occasion using Porton Down's very own employees, some of who were willing to gauge the varying effects for themselves. That situation changed significantly in the final days of 1964. That was when one of the most notorious periods in the history of mind-altering experimentation on military personnel occurred. And it all happened across approximately a period of a week. The work was undertaken and overseen by Porton Down scientists. The projects were code-named *Small Change, Moneybags* and *Recount.*

Much of the experimentation was conducted out in the field. Literally, at times. Military personnel from 41 Royal Marine Commando were the guinea-pigs; although, they were all – technically-speaking - volunteers. The full and potential extents of the effects, however, were most assuredly *not* made fully clear to the troops. Not a surprise. On the first day, the men who were involved took part in an operation that was located not at all far from Porton Down: woods and fields dominated the environment where the experiment began. No LSD was present that day; this was simply just an exercise to have the soldiers get used to the environment. They performed as one would expect trained military men to perform: perfectly. On the next day, however, things were very different and far from perfect. Dosed with LSD, and wholly against their knowledge, things quickly became chaotic for the troops – and that's putting it mildly. The whole project turned into a complete Bedlam.

One of the most important parts of all this is that the events of the second day were carefully filmed – for posterity and to see how quickly, and radically, the men fell under the influence of LSD. It wasn't long before the first symptoms began to kick in: men began to stumble around, they had problems walking. Others began to laugh for no reason – and to levels that could only be described as hysterics. A soldier clambered up a tree. The reason? He wanted to feed the local birds. Another volunteer took a shovel to a tree and almost cut straight though the trunk. One of the men in the film appears to be on the verge of plunging into a full-blown panic-attack. He looks haunted, twitchy and scared. At one point we see him sitting, looking dazed and confused, in a military vehicle. At the same time, a clearly concerned nurse holds his hand. The footage is both gripping and surreal.

MEMORY AND IMPAIRMENT

All of this clearly mirrors key portions of the Rendlesham tests: the 1964 events involved scientists from Porton Down undertaking secret experiments on military personnel. Most significant of all: the Royal Marines had not been told of what was about to happen to them. This is *exactly* what Georgina Bruni told me one of her sources said happened at Rendlesham Forest: the men had no real idea of what awaited them. But, they soon found out. There are clearly other, additional similarities, too: the 1964 experiments on the troops went ahead in woods – as did the 1980 occurrences. When hit by the drugs, some of the men who took part in the 1960s-era tests soon found they couldn't walk properly. In Nick Pope's *Encounter in Rendlesham Forest*, he said Jim Penniston and John Burroughs suddenly found it "difficult to walk properly and they described the experience as being akin to wading through deep water." There was "something seriously wrong," Pope stated. No shit, Sherlock. Burroughs said of the third night of activity: "I have no recall of it. I have no memory of what happened."

On the matter of memory, Deana Fedaie – in an article on the effects of LSD – says: "Cognitive effects include disturbed thought processes, difficulty in thought expression, impairment in reasoning, *and impairment of memory, especially in the integration of short term-memory to long-term memory* [italics mine]."

Andy Roberts, in his important book, *Albion Dreaming: A Popular History of LSD in Britain*, says of those 1964 tests: "Using the term 'volunteer' to describe those who took part in LSD experiments at Porton Down is actually a misnomer. None of the participants was told what drug they would be taking, or what its effects might be. In reality the 'volunteers' were all dupes, conned into taking a powerful mind-altering chemical in strange and unfamiliar circumstances. Porton Down scientists seem to have chosen to ignore the Nuremberg Code for human experimentation, failing to ensure that the volunteers gave informed consent before the tests."

In light of Andy's words, I see no reason as to why Porton Down's cold-as-ice scientists would have had *any* qualms about engaging in such reckless activity. They had secretly done it in 1964, so why not sixteen years later with perhaps another hallucinogen, too? Now, we'll take a look at the next stage of the experiments; something that may very well have been unanticipated when matters were given the green light to "Go."

8

"ARMY ENGINEERS MISCALCULATED THE PREVAILING WINDS"

The genesis of this part of the story dates back to 1986. That was the year in which the late Graham Birdsall – who ran the popular and successful U.K.-based *UFO Magazine* – had a notable conversation with a man named George Wild. Back in the eighties, Wild was employed as a prison officer at a facility called Armley Prison. Built in the 19th century, and located in Leeds, England, it is a "Class C" jail, which means the prisoners are considered those who "cannot be trusted in open conditions but who are unlikely to try to escape."

George Wild quietly confided in Birdsall something highly disturbing, something he had learned from a fellow officer: on the night of December 27, 1980, the U.K. government's Home Office was hastily readying local law-enforcement personnel to evacuate several prisons in Suffolk. Wild said he knew for sure one of the prisons was HM [Her Majesty's] Prison Highpoint North. It is situated in the village of Stradishall, Suffolk, which is approximately forty-four miles from Woodbridge.

As for the primary role of the Home Office, its staff state: "The first duty of the government is to keep citizens safe and the country secure. The Home Office has been at the front line of this endeavor since 1782. As such, the Home Office plays a fundamental role in the security and economic prosperity of the United Kingdom."

The inference was that the planned evacuations were due to what was happening at Rendlesham Forest. As we shall soon see, there is further data that supports this particular scenario.

BEHIND CLOSED DOORS

We've seen that one of those who had a fascination for the Rendlesham Forest mystery was the Admiral of the Fleet Peter John Hill-Norton, Baron Hill-Norton. From 1971 to 1973, he held the position of Chief of the Defense Staff. Having heard of the curious rumors revolving around HM Prison Highpoint North, Hill-Norton was determined to get to the heart of the matter. Unfortunately, Hill-Norton's attempts to pry open the can of worms failed miserably. It was on October 23, 1997 that Hill-Norton brought up the issue in the U.K. government's House of Lords. The response he got was this:

"Lord Hill-Norton asked Her Majesty's Government whether staff at Highpoint Prison in Suffolk received instructions to prepare for a possible evacuation of the prison at some time between 25 and 30 December 1980, and, if so why these instructions were issued."

Lord Williams of Mostyn provided a response that only served to muddy the waters even more: "I regret to advise the noble Lord that I am unable to answer his question, as records for Highpoint Prison relating to the period concerned are no longer available. The governor's journal is the record in which a written note is made of significant events concerning the establishment on a daily basis. It has not proved possible to locate that journal."

As I've stressed, government personnel are very careful when it comes to making statements on sensitive topics. Lord Williams did not deny the story that a major evacuation was almost initiated in late 1980. Instead, he simply said that the logbook for that particular period could not be found. And that was the end of it. Hill-Norton was deeply frustrated by the take-it-or-leave-it response that was dished out to him. You might wonder why someone like Hill-Norton – who was the Chief of the Defense Staff for two years – would not be told the full true story. The answer is actually quite simple: Hill-Norton retired in 1977, three years before the Rendlesham Forest incident even occurred. And it was two decades after his retirement that he demanded answers concerning HM Prison Highpoint North. Hill-Norton – despite his influential and powerful standing in the government and the military in the 1970s – was long out of the loop by the time George Wild had got the ball rolling in the 1980s. By then, Hill-Norton no longer possessed what is known in government as a "need to know." Or, in Hill-Norton's position, a *lack* of a need to know.

HOT GOSSIP ABOUNDS

Our story moves on from HM Prison Highpoint North to another strand of this curious part of Rendlesham. It's a story Georgina Bruni found herself involved in. Bruni confided in me that she had a source of information on the prison connections and who held a significant position in the U.K.'s Special Branch – which, in 2005, was merged into the Metropolitan Police Anti-Terrorist Branch (SO13). Counter Terrorism Command now performs the roles Special Branch previously performed. According to what Georgina was told, one of the other prisons primed for evacuation was HM Prison Blundeston, located thirty-nine miles from Woodbridge. Opened in the early 1960s, it once housed around five hundred prisoners. In 2013, an announcement was made by the Home Office that the jail was to be closed no later than 2014.

Bruni's Special Branch whistleblower informed her the other jail was HM Prison Hollesley Bay. The U.K. government's HM Prison & Probation Service says of the facility: "Hollesley Bay opened on this site as a Borstal in 1938. From that year and until 2006, the prison managed an 1800 acre farm on which the care of both crops and livestock, delivered employment for the prisoners. Today the establishment is an outward looking modern institution which holds sentenced adult males from 18 years and upwards without limit. The farm has gone, and a focus on resettlement and reducing re-offending is at the heart of our agenda. The establishment has developed a strong reputation in successfully preparing life sentenced prisoners for their final release."

It should be noted HM Prison Hollesley is barely eight miles from the village of Woodbridge.

The aforementioned Lord Hill-Norton attempted to get to the heart of this – as he did with the matter of HM Prison Highpoint North – but completely failed. Even he couldn't succeed in forcing open the doors behind which the secrets of Rendlesham Forest were held. It was on January 23, 2001 that Hill-Norton pressed for answers on the matter of those planned evacuations. The response came from Lord Bassam, who, at the time, was the Parliamentary Under-Secretary of State for the Home Office. Lord Bassam's reply ran to just nine words: "We can find no record of any such instructions."

They were tactful, carefully chosen words, to say the least.

BEHIND BARS

It's interesting to note that Jenny Randles has revealed something that may be connected to all of this. In July 1985, Randles was approached by a man who she called "Tommy Doyle." Randles chose to give the man a pseudonym because, at the time, he was in prison. For burglary. Doyle wrote to Jenny, after he read *Sky Crash*; a copy of which just happened to be in the prison library. Doyle claimed knowledge of the Rendlesham incident. He even claimed possession of a certain secret file on the controversy. It was said to have been a file that was confiscated by prison officials when it was found that Doyle had it. Randles was open-minded on what Doyle had to say, but understandably guarded, too. She received one phone call from Doyle after he completed his sentence some months later – and that was it. No more communication. Of course, relying on the words of a burglar might not be the wisest thing to do. There are, however, a couple of points that do make me wonder on the scenario of Doyle knowing at least something of the activity in the forest.

First, there's the fact that Doyle was definitely in prison. We know that because Jenny corresponded with him by mail and while he was still behind bars. And, we also know – thanks to Georgina Bruni, Graham Birdsall and George Wild – that there was a significant prison-based connection to the whole case. Could Doyle have learned something about that prison link to the 1980 incidents while he, himself, was incarcerated? Maybe so. The reason I say that is for the following reason: the prison in which Doyle was held was situated in Norfolk, England. And Norfolk just happens to border Suffolk – the county where the Rendlesham activity occurred. Randles' correspondence with Tommy Doyle occurred one year before George Wild spoke to Graham Birdsall about what he knew of this prison connection to the case. And it was three years before Birdsall decided to reveal Wild's words in his – Birdsall's - magazine. In light of that, I consider it at least a possibility Doyle could have had some degree of awareness of what happened back in December 1980, even though his background causes problems when it comes to the matter of credibility.

"ARMY ENGINEERS MISCALCULATED
THE PREVAILING WINDS"

I have seriously pondered on what is admittedly a controversial scenario: there may have been a worrying possibility that the hallucinogens released in the woods by the Porton Down team had spread further than was originally planned. Or, at least, those same hallucinogens had the potential to do so. They might have reached HM Hollesley Bay – hence the reason for a potential evacuation. The distance from Woodbridge to the prison is just a few miles. It's possible some of the planned evacuations didn't just revolve around Suffolk's prisons. There may have been *additional* experiments, also using hallucinogens, and that took place on the same night, but in different locations to Rendlesham Forest. That is entirely plausible. In fact, we have information that absolutely supports that particular picture. You will recall there was the matter of those men wearing hazmat gear who were seen at RAF Watton...*in the same timeframe and late at night.* In the same way that an experiment was initiated close to the old Bentwaters-Woodbridge facilities, perhaps another one took place near RAF Watton. That would make perfect sense, as the distance from Watton to the forest is roughly forty miles. There's no way that hallucinogens released in Rendlesham Forest would have drifted that far to RAF Watton. It's interesting to note there's a potential precedent to this issue of hazards concerning hallucinogens. That precedent, incredibly, *also* has a UFO connection to it. That connection concerns one of the most famous of all UFO cases of the 20th century.

In the latter stages of the Second World War, the U.S. military used Horn Island, Mississippi, as a place where top secret, biological-warfare research could be undertaken. Matters were brought to an end when the Second World War was over. The official line is that research in the area was cancelled. There are, however, local tales of covert operations and experiments into mind-manipulation in the region as late as the early 1970s. In terms of what may have been used in these island-based operations, knowing fingers carefully point in the direction of Buzz, which, recall, has a tie to the works of both Porton Down and the Edgewood Arsenal. We now get to the heart of the matter of the evacuations angle.

H.P. Albarelli, Jr.'s 2009 book, *A Terrible Mistake*, tells the story of the death in November 1953 of Frank Olson. He was a chemist who, up until his untimely ending, worked as a biochemist with the U.S. Army on secret programs designed to create mind-altering cocktails. Albarelli, Jr., says that at least some of the planned operations at Horn Island didn't work at all well because *"Army engineers miscalculated the prevailing winds which blew eight months of the year toward the mainland's populated areas* [italics mine]."

See where I'm going with all of this? As a Brit, I can tell you with unswerving accuracy that the cold North Sea winds can be absolutely bone-chilling near the Suffolk coast. Powerful, too. There is a very interesting story that few know about, but that may be relevant to the above. Still on this matter, there's a story that surfaced on July 31, 1994. The source of the story? None other than Charles Halt. In a lecture at the city of Leeds, U.K., he revealed that only a few hours after the first night of activity in the woods, a C141 *Starlifter* aircraft, which was used in operations *Desert Shield* and *Desert Storm*, arrived. A number of what were intriguingly termed "special individuals" exited the plane and made their quick way to the East Gate of RAF Woodbridge. Not even Halt knew what was going on. The team was in the woods for a number of hours, after which they left the woods, took their seats on the plane, and got the hell out of Dodge. Georgina Bruni theorized to me the team may have been there to remove any and all materials relative to the deployment of the hallucinogens the night before. Yes, it was only a scenario on the part of one of Georgina's informants, but, it certainly made a lot of sense.

ANOTHER "ALIEN ENCOUNTER" THAT PROBABLY WASN'T ONE AT ALL

Still on this matter, October 11, 1973 was the date of the famous alien abduction of Charles Hickson and Calvin Parker at Pascagoula, Mississippi, by strange, humanoid creatures that had crab- or lobster-like claws. The case has become a classic in Ufology. Not many know, though, that barely a few miles away from where Parker and Hickson were allegedly taken by aliens is… *Horn Island.* In light of that startling fact, we might want to consider the possibility that the Hickson-Parker alien abduction may not have been what it seemed to have been. Just like Rendlesham, it could have been an ingeniously staged event that turned innocent members of the public into victims of people who utterly lacked consciences. The Pascagoula kidnapping - by scientists rather than by aliens - however, is something for another day. Maybe, even, for another book. I'll have to think about that one. Carefully.

There's another angle to the Rendlesham experiments, too, that we will look at. We've addressed the issues of controlled ball lightning, the Porton Down connection, and the possibility of some of the military personnel having had their minds messed with by hallucinogens. The next part of the story involves the utilization of hologram-based technology that was designed to deceive – even more - those same personnel who were targeted by the crazed overseers of the projects.

9

"THIS HAS REALLY TAKEN A TOLL ON HIM"

Ray Boeche is a long-term, respected UFOlogist and an Anglican priest who makes his home in Lincoln, Nebraska. He is also one of the key figures in the Rendlesham riddle – and particularly so in connection to the "top secret experiment" angle of the case. Ray's bloodhound-like persistence and tenacity – when it came to his very own investigation of the Bentwaters-Woodbridge mystery – plunged him into a strange and even disturbing world. Shadowy Department of Defense whistleblowers, an American politician who quickly found himself in way over his head as he carefully looked into the case, tales of hidden military programs, and the possible clandestine surveillance of Boeche himself, were just the start of things. Sounds like something straight out of *The X-Files*, right? Yep. Except for one, huge, glaring thing: the on-screen adventures of Mulder and Scully were fiction. What Boeche uncovered was conspiracy-filled fact.

I have known Ray Boeche since 2007. That was the year in which I extensively interviewed him for my book, *Final Events*. It tells a highly intriguing story of how and why there are powerful figures in the Pentagon who believe that the UFO phenomenon is demonic – rather than extraterrestrial – in nature. Boeche and I stayed in touch after the *Final Events* interviews were, well, finalized. And to this day we still chat. When I decided I was going to write *The Rendlesham Forest UFO Conspiracy*, I reached out to Ray, primarily because I knew he had a great deal to say on the mysterious matter. He was more than happy to help. In fact, as well as granting me an interview, Ray very generously provided me with a PDF file of his original notes and correspondence concerning his Rendlesham investigations – all of which occurred back in the 1980s.

"WHY WON'T YOU LEAVE HIM ALONE?"

"My first connection with it," Ray said to me, "was with a conference I organized for the University of Nebraska with Scott Colborn. This would be 1983. We brought in Jenny Randles and Dot Street. Then, as we started, we tried to get a hold of Adrian Bustinza, and talked to him a time or two. And Scott talked to him once by himself. Adrian's response was genuinely frightened. He had been really disturbed by this.

"One time I tried to call and get a hold of Adrian, but got a hold of his mom. She really read me the riot act and said: 'Adrian couldn't sleep and this was really disturbing him. Why won't you leave him alone?' In no uncertain terms, she made it very clear that he was really struggling. It was after we tried to reach out to Adrian and got this response that we focused more on: where do we go from here? And that moved us toward Senator Jim Exon." Politics and the world of the unexplained were about to come together – and in a truly strange way. [Author's note: Until his death on March 30, 2020, Scott Colborn had a regular Saturday morning radio show that was broadcasted out of Lincoln, Nebraska. Its title: *Exploring Unexplained Phenomena*].

"MILITARY RESEARCH AND DEVELOPMENT...
STRATEGIC AND CRITICAL MATERIALS"

As for who, exactly, Senator Exon was, well, that is a story all of its own. A well-respected Democrat, Exon was the governor of Nebraska from 1971 to 1979, and the senator for Nebraska from 1979 to 1997. Exon was also a key member of the U.S. Senate Committee on Armed Services, specifically the chairman of the subcommittee.

As the committee, itself, shows: "The Senate Committees on Military Affairs; on the Militia; and Naval Affairs were established on December 10, 1816. The Committee on the Militia was merged with the Committee on Military Affairs in 1858 to form the Military Affairs and Militia Committee. However, in 1872 the Committee dropped 'Militia' from its name. The Military Affairs and Naval Affairs Committees existed until 1947 when they were combined by the Legislative Reorganization Act of 1946 into a new standing committee, the current Committee on Armed Services."

The committee has had jurisdiction over various areas for many years, including: "Aeronautical and space activities peculiar to or primarily associated with the development of weapons systems or military operations;" "Department of Defense, the Department of the Army, the Department of the Navy, and the Department of the Air Force, generally;" "military research and development;" and "strategic and critical materials necessary for the common defense."

Exon was, without a doubt, someone whose work impacted significantly on matters relative to national security.

"I AM NOT CONVINCED"

It was in the early months of 1985 that Boeche decided to take his investigation to the next level: namely, to seek help from Senator Exon. Ultimately, things didn't go quite as well as Boeche had hoped for. There is no doubt at all, however, that the whole situation touched a highly sensitive nerve within the labyrinthine corridors of power. Boeche put out a notable feeler to the Senator, as Boeche told me: "We got him a copy of *Sky Crash* and *Clear Intent*. [The latter] contained six-pages of material on the case, and we sent those to Exon's office. A copy of the Halt tape, too. And that started the entire thing."

On March 18, 1985, Exon wrote to Ray: "As you requested, I have asked the Air Force for their assistance. Please know that when I hear from them, I will be back in touch. I am still reviewing the two books you provided me, Mr. Boeche. I will return them when I have finished."

Ray received another response from Exon on April 2. Exon came straight to the point: "Frankly, I am not convinced that the incidents you are concerned with did, in fact, occur. Nor have I found any evidence of a cover-up by the government." Exon did, however, inform Boeche that he had contacted the Air Force, the National Academy of Science, and NASA, and would keep Boeche appraised of any and all replies that came his way.

Then, on the afternoon of April 10, Boeche had a phone-based conversation with Lieutenant Colonel Halt. Boeche's handwritten notes – copies of which are in my hands – state that: "Halt said he would be willing to discuss the case with Exon, and would be glad to answer any of his questions. I asked Halt about the existence of soil samples. He said, 'Yes, soil samples were taken; as a matter of fact I have one here on my desk.'"

Boeche's notes continue: "I asked about plaster casts and he responded, 'Yes, plaster casts were made of the landing impressions.' I asked if he had those also, and he replied, 'No, I don't have them here, but I know where I can put my hands on them in short order.'"

"WE KNOW NOTHING ABOUT THIS"

Ray's concise and wholly valid response to Exon's "I am not convinced" statement went like this: "We have verified documents. So how can you say they didn't take place?" A very good question, indeed. "At one point," Boeche said to me, "I was also in touch with Exon's defense aide in Washington. I received this enormous package of just boilerplate crap from the Air Force and various other agencies they had sent to Exon saying there's nothing to this. 'We know nothing about this,' they were saying. But the interesting thing is that at the time, our phone number was unlisted. We were not in the city directory. And, my mail correspondence came to a post office box. Not to my home address. And I had never given my home address to Senator Exon or any of his people or aides.

"I immediately called Exon's Washington office and spoke with him. And I just said: 'I just got a whole package of responses from the Senator, none of which are really responsive. And all of which I've received in some form or other from various agencies.' And I said to him: 'My big question to you is this: why did this come to my home address? As far as I'm concerned, you guys don't have my home address. It's not publicly available.' And he started to hem and haw: 'Er, er, er. Well, we have a file on you that's just huge. And, I imagine somehow that your address came into that.'

"I thought: well, that's interesting. I actually filed a FOIA request with the FBI to see if they had a file on me. They said they didn't have anything responsive. I didn't pursue it too much after that. It could have been various agencies: AFOSI, CIA, all kinds of agencies. [The aide] didn't know what Exon had found out. He was not involved in any of the investigations. He said: 'Senator Exon made all his own phone calls, arranged and attended all of the meetings with various people involved.' Not the staff, he did it all himself. And he said: 'That's really unusual for the senator to put so much time and effort into it. I know he has talked to Colonel Halt. I know he's talked with virtually everyone in the Department of Defense, but I can't give you any details because he's done it all himself.'"

"ADDITIONAL INFORMATION OTHER THAN THAT YOU HAVE OBTAINED MAY EXIST"

On June 13, Senator Exon sent another letter to Boeche. Exon made two notable statements in that same piece of correspondence. One read: "From this recent effort, and my responses to your previous inquiries, I believe that I have investigated all possible avenues within the Federal Government." Clearly, Exon was trying to curtail his correspondence with Boeche – and as soon as was possible, it seemed.

Exon's second statement said: "While additional information other than that you have obtained may exist, I can find no evidence of a coverup [sic] of UFO incidents by any department or agency of the U.S. Government."

I have to say, I find those words to be particularly intriguing. Exon told Boeche additional material on the Woodbridge-Bentwaters issue "*may* exist." Exon then, however, went on to say that the specific UFO angle had no validity attached to it. That, to me, sounds like Exon was trying to provide Boeche with a clue or two, but not explicitly. Namely, that *yes*, something out of the ordinary *did* happen – and there *was* additional data, if one knew where to look for it – but that it had *nothing* to do with UFOs. Exon's very carefully worded sentence makes me wonder if it was written by an attorney; something designed to protect the Senator's reputation if certain revelations concerning Exon and Rendlesham Forest should have surfaced in the months or years ahead – which, as history has demonstrated, didn't happen.

Back to Ray Boeche:

"WE HAVE REACHED A DEAD END ON THIS"

Ray continued: "About that same time, Phyllis Galde, of *Fate* magazine, contacted me and wanted me to write an article on Bentwaters, so I was working on that. I contacted Exon's Lincoln [Nebraska] office and spoke to Exon's secretary here in Lincoln. I said, 'I would like to make an appointment with the senator next time he's in town, because I'm working on an article for a national magazine. And I want to get his comments on this, and I want to be sure I get it directly from him. And that I'm not just quoting him.' And, boy, she just launched into a tirade. She was literally screaming at me over the phone: 'You are not going to try to pin the senator down in a national magazine; you don't know how much time he's spent on this. This has really taken a toll on him.'

"Her response was just way off the charts. I mean, it was a visceral response. It's certainly not what you would expect from a person who you would think would be as eminently professional as they could, being the spokesperson for the senator. Eventually, she finally slammed the phone down. From what his secretary here in Lincoln said, I got the feeling that Exon had either been warned off or was so disturbed by what he discovered that he just didn't know how to deal with it himself. That was just so curious. And that was pretty much the end of it. No more correspondence;

couldn't connect with him. I exhausted everything I could find from Exon."

On August 14, Exon told Ray that he felt "we have reached a dead end on this," that "I cannot have my staff devoting a disproportionate share of their time to rehash previous time-consuming information that has been checked out," and that "it would not be possible" for the two to meet in person. The senator's final words: "I do hope you recognize that we have put in more staff time on this matter than any other case since I have been a United States Senator."

Things weren't over, however: six years later there was a new development in relation to Rendlesham Forest and Ray Boeche. It got even more conspiratorial.

10

"A WORLD OF TROUBLE"

It's certainly not every day you get to meet with a pair of Edward Snowden-style whistleblowers from the U.S. Department of Defense. But, incredibly, that's *exactly* what happened to Ray Boeche on November 25, 1991. The location, however, was not a dark and shadowy parking garage – as per the story of "Deep Throat" in Bob Woodward's and Carl Bernstein's hit book of 1974, *All the President's Men*. Rather, it was a pleasant restaurant in the Lincoln Marriott Cornhusker Hotel in Lincoln, Nebraska. I guess you've already got a good idea of what the two guys wanted to talk about. Along with various and sundry theories concerning the UFO phenomenon, it was those mysterious woods on the other side of the world and what went down deep within them in December 1980.

Ray told me of those mysterious characters: "I found it interesting they had contacted me at work; and I have no idea how they tracked me down there. But, they wanted to know if we could get together and have lunch to discuss something important. I met them for a brief period of time on that first meeting and then they said: 'We'd like to get together and have a longer conversation.' I arranged a time and it was quite a lengthy discussion, probably three and a half hours. And that's how it all came about. After both meetings, when I was able to verify the men held the degrees they claimed to hold, and were apparently who they claimed to be, I was intrigued and excited at the possibility of having stumbled on a more or less untouched area which could be researched. But, I was also cautious in terms of 'why me?'"

Both men were physicists, recalled Boeche, probably in their late forties or early fifties back then, and were "involved in areas of research I would find interesting." Who could resist a tantalizing lure like that? Certainly not Ray. He said: "Most of it was related to psychotronic weaponry." And, it all went from there directly to a discussion on Rendlesham. As Boeche sat and listened, an astounding and alarming story came tumbling out.

Of psychotronic weapons, the *Washington Post* stated in January 2007: "In 2002, the Air Force Research Laboratory patented precisely such a technology: using microwaves to send words into someone's head...Rich Garcia, a spokesman for the research laboratory's directed energy directorate, declined to discuss that patent or current or related research in the field, citing the lab's policy not to comment on its microwave work. In response to a Freedom of Information Act request filed for this article, the Air Force released unclassified documents surrounding that 2002 patent - records that note that the patent was based on human experimentation in October 1994 at the Air Force lab, where scientists were able to transmit phrases into the heads of human subjects, albeit with marginal intelligibility. Research appeared to continue at least through 2002. Where this work has gone since is unclear — the research laboratory, citing classification, refused to discuss it or release other materials."

"THIS WAS SOME SORT OF PSYCHOTRONIC
DEVICE, A HOLOGRAM"

"I found it interesting that they would mention Rendlesham at the meeting," Ray recalled. *"They said there was a sense that this was maybe, in some sense, staged. Or, that some of the senior people there were more concerned with the reaction of the men, how they responded to the situation, rather than what was actually going on.* That this was some sort of psychotronic device - *a hologram* - to see what sort of havoc they can wreak with people. But, even if it was a type of hologram, *they said it could interact with the environment.* The tree marks and the pod marks at the landing site were indications of that. But how can you have a projected thing like a hologram that also has material, physical capabilities? They wouldn't elaborate on this [italics mine]."

Boeche, however, *did* expand on this: "The Bentwaters-Rendlesham event was an experiment. It was a projection of a three-dimensional object, but it had the ability to interact with the environment. A hologram with solidity. Or that *could* have solidity."

As I listened, Ray Boeche's account added yet further weight to the theory that Rendlesham was a government experiment. As an aside, he told me he had heard of the Porton Down connection to the incidents in the forest as far back as the early 1980s – long before me, Nick Pope or Georgina Bruni had even a slight awareness of the link.

With a degree of noticeable frustration in his voice, Ray concluded to me: "There are so many possibilities. Any theory you pick, any explanation you choose, you can find evidence to support it. It's maddening because there's nothing absolutely definitive out there. I'm convinced there was interaction with some sort of phenomenon, in light of what those DoD guys told me. So, there was some sort of physical object that left traces in the environment. But it was projected. That was the word they used: *projected* [italics mine]."

"HIGH LEVEL PEOPLE"

Ray came away from the meeting amazed: was the information provided to him the literal truth? Or, was he fed far more than a liberal amount of disinformation? Questions whirled around his head – as they naturally would! Now, we come to another important question: Why, specifically, was it Boeche who was contacted by that mysterious pair from the DoD? An answer came in 1994, around three years after that strange meeting. On this particular point, it's important to note Ray was not the only person in the UFO research community who had communication with the mysterious duo. So did Linda Howe. On one occasion, they told her, in no uncertain terms: "We had become aware of [Ray Boeche] through his work on the British incident (Bentwaters Dec. 26-28, 1980), when his probings began to bother a number of high level people within our government."

One really has to wonder if those "high level people" included certain sources in the U.S. Senate Committee on Armed Services. Maybe, even, none other than Senator Exon, himself. He didn't retire from politics until 1997; three years after Linda Howe was contacted in 1994. That Boeche was told to tread very carefully was something his two sources stressed to him. The two men had some slightly sinister final words for Ray: "We don't want this traced back to us. If you were to start asking about these projects you would be in a world of trouble, just for being aware of the [project] names."

To his credit, Ray was not deterred by this potentially dangerous situation. He continues his work in the field of Ufology to this very day. It wasn't just Ray, however, who pursued this hologram angle.

"THE RESULT IS A TERRIFYING APPARITION"

Jenny Randles had a good, solid, working relationship with Ray Boeche. She, too, addressed the matter of what Boeche's secret informants told him back in 1991. On the matter of those claims pertaining to highly sophisticated holograms, Jenny stated: "This is a device which manipulates the subatomic basis of matter at a quantum level and builds a bridge between mind and physical substance. If I understood it correctly, this supposedly stimulated the mind into having vivid hallucinations but, at the same time, created physical effects in the real world which could take on a semblance of the appearance of the hallucinated images. What was seen was mostly in the mind – but it was not entirely without physical form and partially substantial in the same way that a hologram is real, but has no weight or solidity. The result is a terrifying apparition."

"RESEARCH WHICH INVOLVED QUANTUM THEORY"

We've seen how, over the years, Georgina Bruni provided me with various data that related to a connection between the Rendlesham Forest experiment and scientists at Porton Down. Bruni was certainly not a full-on believer in the theory that the incidents in the woods were nothing but the results of top-secret human experimentation. She stressed to me she viewed the hologram angle as a theory to be studied. Georgina was, though, incredibly generous with her information on this angle - and quite open to sharing with me what she found concerning a secret domestic explanation for Rendlesham. Even if she didn't fully buy into it, Georgina was happy to help when and where she could.

In 1998, Georgina suggested to me that as well as looking into the matter of the Porton Down angle, I should also address the hologram-driven theory. The reason was because she felt there just might have been a possibility that the two were somehow interconnected. If you were to mix hallucinogens from Porton Down with military-created holograms – and add a degree of laser-guided ball lightning, too – from the perspective of the manipulated men in the woods it would have resulted in a spectacular double-whammy of tumultuous proportions.

Not only did Georgina make that aforementioned suggestion: in January 2000 she mailed me a typed document that outlined her thoughts on all of this – and which, to a far greater degree, appeared later in her November 2000 book, *You Can't Tell the People*. In opening, she wrote to me, quoting from that same document: "According to Ray Boeche's visitors, the Americans were studying Fourier's transforms and David Bohm's contemporary research which involved quantum theory."

The *Continuum Center* states of the work of Bohm, a theoretical physicist who died in 1992: "Bohm suggests that the mental and the physical sides, which he sees as two 'poles' of a unified whole, are closely interlinked and that 'at each level, information is the bridge or link between the two sides.' A relationship between the mental and matter may exist at indefinitely great levels of subtlety, while nonetheless each kind and level of mind may have a relative autonomy and stability."

This "mental and matter"-based top secret research apparently allowed those handling the program to quite literally give temporary physical substance to something that was created in – and interpreted in the depths of - the imagination. If it was a UFO you were primed to see, that's what would manifest in hologram form. In many respects, this is not at all too dissimilar to the Tibetan concept of what are known as Tulpas and thought-forms. As I noted in my 2017 book, *The Slenderman Mysteries*: "In essence, it is the process by which the human mind can allegedly bring some degree of alternative, physical existence to an entity that is created solely within the depths of the imagination - and from within the dream state, too. And as unlikely as it may sound, each and every one of us may well possess the ability to give 'life' to certain 'things' that don't exist in the same way that we do. "

"WAS THE UFO SOME KIND OF HOLOGRAM?"

Georgina Bruni said to me that Ray Boeche's informants "explained that holography and Fourier transforms are a way of separating an image from its object, the viewing of the image at a distance. In essence, they claim the world is a hologram composed of interference patterns that can be altered by disruptive static frequencies. They believe the human brain is part of this hologram and as such it is capable of performing its own Fourier transforms. However, they concluded that the human brain is unreliable, whereas a psychotronic device, much like a computer, would be able to exert an exact effect on animate and inanimate objects."

Georgina had much more to impart. In her raw notes mailed to me, she said: "If the Americans were attempting to electronically recognize frequency interference patterns in space with the aim of transforming the desired Fourier components into holographic images of a kind, could this have been what was seen in Rendlesham Forest? Was the UFO some kind of hologram? This is obviously what the researchers wanted Ray Boeche to believe. They informed him that every avenue was being explored and that the 'Bentwaters experiment,' the projection of a three-dimensional object which interacted with its environment, was created and controlled by individuals involved in this field of research.

"According to the researchers, the idea was to operate a psychotronic device by performing Fourier transforms on background radiation, which would be more reliable when used with a laser.

The airborne laser would be capable of observing everything from electrons moving in silicon chips to the depths of the oceans. Such a device would be able to capture the interference patterns and computerize the imaging. The receiver could decode the components of entire buildings, landscapes and individuals."

Bruni wrote something to me in her document to me that was very notable, and which echoes something we learned earlier: "Interestingly, Colonel Halt's patrol recorded background radiation. Halt has always insisted that during the incident a pencil-thin beam hit the ground just a few feet away from where he was positioned. Supposing this really was an experiment, and the beam was a laser, but then what would be the purpose of creating such a bizarre scenario on the perimeter of a NATO installation? Why would the Americans carry out such a test on foreign soil?"

As for the combined answers to those two questions, Georgina cited a U.K. *Mail on Sunday* newspaper article from 1997 titled "An Army of Ghosts to Spook the Foe." Georgina said: "The newspaper's Washington correspondent reported that *the Pentagon were perfecting a laser which would project holographic decoys* of troops and tanks in order to trick the enemy into thinking it was a real force [italics mine]."

"ONCE THE STORY STARTED THEY LET IT CONTINUE"

Clearly, exposing military personnel to advanced hologram-based technology in those woods, and late at night, would have been a perfect way of gauging just how successfully the manufactured visions had achieved their goals. Those goals were: the creation of holographic UFOs that could interact with not just the environment, but with those who were in its presence, too. "Steve Roberts," one of the very earliest on-base sources who secretly liaised with the Butler-Randles-Street team, said something brief but notable that may be relevant to this matter: "Some of those new to the force thought it was a UFO. Once the story started they let it continue. Of course, it *was* a UFO to them because they had never seen anything like it before."

In this chapter, we have addressed the words, concepts and theories of Ray Boeche, Jenny Randles and Georgina Bruni. We'll close this same chapter with the thoughts of another renowned UFO investigator, Jacques Vallee. He too suggests Rendlesham was a piece of pure, deceptive theater: "The Bentwaters case is a classic. At the landing site, they had a mix of ordinary guards, officers, sentries and so on - they all had orders to go to the site under a scenario. And that's not what would have happened if the encounter were real - if a strange object landed on the base you wouldn't be sending out a hundred people without weapons. *The thing has all the earmarks of being staged for the benefit of the witnesses*, so that they could be studied and the reactions of the different psychological types and of different ranks could be studied. And when you think about it, it's not that weird [italics mine]."

Vallee concluded: "If you were in charge of a project like that, you'd have to test it in conditions where nobody is in danger and you can get the data you need. In cases like this one - not many but a few of them - that I investigated, *I had to conclude that these were tests of virtual reality projectors* [italics mine]."

11

"GHOST AIRCRAFT"

There's yet another issue that comes into play in the story, one that is as fascinating as it is strange: it is that of radar, and of how it became such a notable role in this complicated saga. As for what radar actually is, *ABC Science* provide a concise and clear explanation of what it is and how it works: "One of the key means of tracking the position of aircraft is via radar, a system that evolved before World War II and has been constantly refined since then, explains Dr. Graham Brooker, a radar engineer at the University of Sydney's School of Aerospace, Mechanical and Mechatronic Engineering. The word RADAR is an acronym for RAdio Detection And Ranging, and in its simplest form it consists of a transmitted radio signal aimed by an antenna in a particular direction, and a receiver that detects the echoes off any objects in the path of the signal, he says."

So, how does radar come into play with regard to the incidents that occurred in and around Rendlesham Forest? Well, for years there have been rumors that UFO activity – close to the woods – was picked up by local radar stations and subjected to a high degree of secrecy. Demonstrating that radar was picking up anomalies around the time of the experiments would, for many people, be a clincher when it came to the claim that UFOs were in the skies over Suffolk. But, was that really the case? There's strong evidence that, just like the rest of the Rendlesham story, the radar data was not what it appeared to be. It was yet another example of how those directing the program made sure that every angle was covered. Before we get to the matter of radar and Rendlesham, let's take a look at three UFO-themed, and radar-based, incidents that date back decades. All three are important, as they *seem* to demonstrate proof that aliens can be detected on radar, when that may actually not be the case.

"I WAS, AT THE TIME, A RADAR OPERATOR"

On October 26, 1991, the late J.R. Oliver wrote to UFO author / investigator Timothy Good and related a story worth telling. At the time, I was working on my first book, *A Covert Agenda*. Just over a month later, Tim sent me a copy of Oliver's letter – thinking that I would find it interesting, which I most certainly did. Unfortunately, by the time I wrote to Oliver, he had passed away. His wife, however, very generously gave me permission to use the account of her late husband, and which makes for fascinating reading. Oliver began…

"In August 1949, in order to test the updated air defenses of England against attack, Operation Bulldog was launched. Operation Bulldog's attacking forces consisted of aircraft of the Benelux countries supported by U.S. air squadrons based on the continent. Flying from various airfields in Holland, France, Belgium and Germany, their objective was to attack London and other prime targets in southern and midland England, without being officially 'downed' by fighter aircraft brought into action by the defensive network of Fighter Command.

"The radar defense chain extended from Land's End, along the south coast and up to the north of Scotland, overlapping at all heights from sea level to about 100,000 feet. Even so long ago, it was almost impossible to fly a glider across the Channel without it being plotted. The exercise ran for fifteen days and was structured in such a way that the technical resources and personnel of the defensive screen were stretched to the limit."

Oliver continued: "I was, at the time, a radar operator AC1, stationed at RAF Sandwich in Kent, a Ground Control Interception station, used to verbally direct fighter aircraft onto target aircraft by means of radar guidance and radio transmission. In conjunction with neighboring radar stations, our function, especially during Bulldog, was a busy one. As can be appreciated, air and sea traffic in the vicinity of the Channel tended to be heavier than in other areas of the UK and this reflected in the general high performance of radar stations in that area. All personnel at RAF Sandwich were fully skilled and right on top of their job. Two watches were kept, A and B, on alternate twelve-hour shifts for the duration of Bulldog. About a week into the exercise, after a few hours of being busy, we were stood down, about midnight. Things had gone slack and 'Group' had advised is that we could take a break. This was in the normal run of things during the exercise and except for one radar operator to keep general watch and one other to man the PBX, there was a general move into the small canteen across the corridor."

"IT ABRUPTLY TURNED NORTH"

It wasn't long at all before something very weird occurred as Oliver noted in his letter: "Within about fifteen minutes, the PBX operator came in, approached the Duty Controller and advised him that Bethe first to see the contact and my plot was the first to go on the plot board. As other operators took their positions, more plots were called out concerning position of the object and its height. The object was flying roughly parallel with the south coast, from west to east. Reaching a point out to see off the 'heel' of Kent, it abruptly turned north and as it approached the Thames estuary we passed it on to Martlesham radar, with whom we had been in contact via the PBX link, and whose radar area impinged on our own. Shortly after, we lost contact with it, due to the limit of our own radar range."

Oliver then noted something even more astounding: "It was a simple matter to assess the speed of the object from the times and distances between plots and its height was directly read from our Type 13 radar, designed to read the height of any aircraft within its range. Flying at close to 50,000 feet, the air speed of the object we had observed and plotted in accordance with RAF standard procedures was assessed at very nearly *3,000 miles per hour* [italics mine]."

"The general consensus regarding its size, among the very experienced radar personnel engaged in the operations, was that the object offered an echo similar to that of *a large passenger or freighter surface vessel,* something in the region of *15,000 or 20,00 tons* [italics mine]. Word filtered down that on approaching Bempton radar in Yorkshire, the object suddenly increased speed and headed directly upwards, vanished off-screen at about 100,000 feet."

That was hardly the end of the story, however. In fact, there was more to come. *Much* more.

"FORGET ESPECIALLY THE ODD CIRCUMSTANCES OF THE PAST NIGHT"

Back to Oliver: "Naturally, there was quite a bit of a buzz about this, especially as at that time speeds in excess of the speed of sound were just not on. Neither were aircraft the size of liners. The airspeed record at that time stood at 606.36 mph and the largest aircraft in general use was probably the USAAF *Superfortress*, which lumbered along at about 350 mph. At our usual relief time 'B' Watch stood down and went to breakfast and bed at the domestic site at Stonar House. We were awakened from our watch slumbers by Sergeant Platt and assembled in front of Stonar House, with our Sergeant Belcher, Sergeant Hatter, and various minor NCOs [Non-Commissioned Officers] in attendance, for an address by Squadron Leader Mundy."

Oliver went on to reveal what, exactly, Squadron Leader Mundy had to say about this extraordinary situation: "He reminded us of our duties as serving members of the RAF and the requirements of the OSA [Official Secrets Act] and to forget especially the odd circumstances of the past night and not to mention same to anyone not connected to the RAF. Going on watch that evening we found that the Duty Watch Book, normally only replaced when completely full, which recorded every air engagement, every PBX message, every official order by the watch-keeping officer, made during every official part of previous watches, including the previous night's activities, as an official Watch Book is required to do *had gone* [italics mine]. Replaced by a brand new shining Duty Watch Book. I wonder why? Removing a half empty Watch Book was unheard of, during exercises such as Bulldog especially."

"THIS INCIDENT WAS OBSERVED BY SUCH A LARGE AND HIGHLY TRAINED AUDIENCE"

Oliver continued with his account: "The rest of the exercise took its natural course and about a month later my service with the RAF ended. Whether there were any further developments regarding this incident I do not know but it seems likely that evidence of its happening must be on file somewhere. This incident was observed by such a large and highly trained audience, its progress so well documented and meticulously recorded and, no doubt, the technical aspects so well scrutinized by top-ranking experts that the official documentation of its occurrence would settle the UFO controversy permanently."

Oliver's final words: "All aspects of Operation Bulldog were due to be analyzed in great depth in order to bring our defense against possible nuclear attack to the highest level. There is no doubt that the incident I have described went totally beyond the expectations of the organizing authorities as it must have been, would receive the closest scrutiny and that many opinions must have been placed on record. In addition to the personnel directly involved in the tracking of the object, it is highly likely that a good many people must have gained knowledge of this occurrence and thereof proof of it happening may not be too far in hiding."

"IT WAS VERY HUSH-HUSH"

William Maguire, who enlisted in the Royal Air Force in 1950, told me in a personal interview: "From the early part of 1950, I did my basic training for a few months, and the rest of the year I did technical training and worked on radar and became an instructor. By 1951 I was operative at RAF Sennen, near Land's End in Cornwall. I was a junior NCO [Author's Note: Non-Commissioned Officer], a corporal; but at the time of this incident in 1952, I was a senior aircraftsman; I was on the sports committee and helped edit the station magazine. Most of my five years in the RAF was peace and quiet.' Maguire's military career was not *all* peace and quiet, however.

"We were like a fire-fighting service. We would be called out to go to different RAF stations when they required an accurate reading of their radar instruments from experienced people. So, I was all over the damned place. Usually, it was made clear to us where we were going. You'd get a travel warrant and there's a truck waiting and usually it's got windows you can see out of; but in this case they were closed. Well, we were driven to a location which I believe was very close to RAF Sandwich in Kent and this was night-time. I'd been to Sandwich before, but the actual location was just a field – sort of nowhere."

"THIS ENORMOUS THING"

"I have a feeling that this particular place is not in any book," Maguire said. "It was very hush-hush. The machinery looked quite standard – all to do with detection and observation – but what *did* surprise me as an experienced radar operator was the extent of the machines. They were able to see right across to Eastern Europe and parts of Russia and way over to Sweden, which I hadn't realized at that time we could do. My memory was that everything was in a complete flap. Normally, in a military situation everything is ordered, regular and set out. But here was a situation that was plainly out of control. Mechanics were flying about all over the place."

As William Maguire got his bearings and the situation was revealed to him in its stark form, however, the reasons behind the blind panic became staggeringly clear. Some form of huge, unidentified aerial object was being tracked on the radar-scopes high over the English Channel. As Maguire reveals, "The mechanics were being blamed for not calibrating the instruments properly; we were being blamed for not interpreting the readings properly. But the obvious answer staring us in the face, on every single instrument on the base, was the fact that there was sitting up at an unbelievable height, this enormous thing with the equivalent mass of a warship and it just stood there…and stood there…and stood there."

That is, until it split into three pieces and quickly vanished into the skies above.

"A SIGHTING OF AN UNUSUAL NATURE"

From now-declassified U.K. Air Ministry files from the 1950s, we have the following story of March 26, 1957. I quote directly from the relevant, original documentation that can be read at the U.K.'s National Archive:

"A report was received from Royal Air Force Church Lawford on 26th March, 1957 of a sighting of an unusual nature. The object moved at a speed timed at exceeding 1400 mph. This in itself was unusual as the object had accelerated to this speed from a stationary position. No explanation has yet been found for this sighting but a supplementary report, including a copy of the radar plot, was requested and has been received from Church Lawford this afternoon."

All three of these incidents, from 1949 to 1957, have several things in common. They all involved expert radar-based personnel. And the "UFOs" were only tracked by radar: *none of the "craft" were ever seen visually*. That latter point is important to understanding the full picture of the radar-Rendlesham crossover. Some might say this suggests the phenomena had the ability to become invisible. I guess such a scenario is not impossible. There is, however, a far more down to earth explanation for all of this strange, radar-based activity in the skies of the U.K. We will come to that explanation very soon. But, first, let's address the matter of radar and Rendlesham Forest.

"THAT IS ALL THE INFORMATION WE HAVE"

Rumors suggest radar tapes were taken from RAF Watton by U.S. Air Force personnel who wanted to examine the alleged UFO evidence and see what, exactly, the tapes showed. This part of the story began in January 1981 with a writer named Paul Begg. It turns out Begg knew a serviceman who was aware of something of the UFO incidents. It wasn't long before Jenny Randles was able to speak with this particular source. Not wanting to jeopardize the man's career, Randles chose to refer to him as "David Potts." It was Potts who was able to put the pieces together.

Potts told Randles that it was on December 29 when the Americans turned up at RAF Watton. Jenny learned they took not just the radar-based data, but even the logbook for the relevant time. There was a very strange facet to all of this: the U.S. agents openly stated to their Royal Air Force counterparts that they needed the radar material because a craft from another world had come down in Rendlesham Forest. And they had orders to secure and scrutinize whatever material was available. While there is no reason at all to think Potts was lying, the fact is that U.S. intelligence operatives simply would not stroll into a U.K. military base and loudly spout off about a crashed UFO. That's not how the military works. And it's certainly not how secrets are kept.

Clearly, and obviously, the Americans were there to further sow the seeds of the UFO story created to hide the truth of the December experiments. No doubt, they knew that those who worked at RAF Watton, and who had been told the story by their American colleagues, would have a hard time keeping quiet on a hot potato like that! And, as history has shown, David Potts did *not* stay quiet. He went on to become a significant figure in the radar-based angle of the story.

While the more sensationalized RAF Watton story has never been vindicated, there is proof that the base was involved to some degree. As I noted earlier, in October 1988 I was informed by Squadron Leader E.E. Webster of RAF Watton: "Our log book for the period does indeed say that a UFO was reported to us by RAF Bentwaters at 0325 GMT on 28 December 1980 but that is all the information we have."

There is, however, more to come.

FURTHER INFORMATION ON RENDLESHAM
FOREST AND RADAR

On October 2, 1983, the *News of the World* newspaper reported that, "The first sighting of the craft over England was recorded on a radar screen" at RAF Watton. The *NOTW* added that, "Radar operators followed the progress as it flew over the East Coast until it disappeared."

Moving ahead, in July 2015 the BBC took a look at the radar-driven side of all this. They told their readers: "New evidence has been gathered to back up claims a UFO landed near a U.S. airbase in Suffolk, a former deputy commander has claimed. Col. Charles Halt told the BBC he saw unidentified objects at Rendlesham Forest in December 1980. He says he now has statements from radar operators at RAF Bentwaters and nearby Wattisham airfield that an unknown object was tracked at the time."

The BBC got to the heart of the matter, as it relates to radar. They quoted Charles Halt as saying: "I have confirmation that (Bentwaters radar operators)... saw the object go across their 60 mile (96km) scope in two or three seconds, thousands of miles an hour. He came back across their scope again, stopped near the water tower, they watched it and observed it go into the forest where we were," said Col Halt. "At Wattisham, they picked up what they called a 'bogie' and lost it near Rendlesham Forest. Whatever was there was clearly under intelligent control."

"TECHNOLOGICAL INNOVATIONS"

With so much data in hand – suggesting that radar played such a significant role in this story – you might say to me: "Isn't this proof that aliens really *were* flying over Suffolk in late December?" I say "No!" Why? Because, there is something that can turn everything on its collective head. It shows how the radar tapes didn't monitor *anything* of a UFO kind. Just like the military personnel in Rendlesham Forest who thought they were encountering something extraterrestrial, those who were working on the radar side of things were also manipulated to accept something that wasn't real. They were led to believe that something strange and unearthly was in the sky when, in all actuality, nothing was caught on radar. It just appeared to be the case. Yet again, things are not what they seem to be – which is just about the theme of this whole story. For the answers to the full picture of this radar issue, we have to study the secret work of S. Eugene Poteat.

SEEING AND TRACKING A GHOST AIRCRAFT

The Institute of World Politics provides background on Poteat: "S. Eugene (Gene) Poteat is a retired senior CIA Scientific Intelligence Officer, and has served as President of the Association of Former Intelligence Officers (AFIO). He was educated as an electrical engineer and physicist. He holds a Masters in Statecraft and National Security Affairs from IWP. His career in intelligence included work with U-2 and SR-71 class of aircraft and various space and naval reconnaissance systems…He received the CIA's Medal of Merit and the National Reconnaissance Office's Meritorious Civilian Award for his technological innovations."

One of those "technological innovations" likely played a big role in trying to convince people that aliens were in the skies of Suffolk.

The Volume 42, No. 1, 1998 edition of *Studies in Intelligence* included a paper written by Poteat. Its title: "Stealth, Countermeasures, and ELINT, 1960-1975." One particularly important and relevant part of Poteat's paper reads like this: "I came up with a scheme to electronically generate and inject carefully calibrated false targets into the Soviet radars, deceiving them into seeing and tracking a ghost aircraft." He continued: "…we could simulate the false target's range and speed. Knowing the radar's power and coverage from the PPMS [Power and Pattern Measurement Systems] projects, *we could now simulate an aircraft of any radar cross section from an invisible stealth plane to one that made a large blip on Soviet radar screens* [italics mine]."

What all of this demonstrates is that the CIA, thanks to Poteat, had the ability to create false readings on radar screens – chiefly to confuse the Russians and to determine the capabilities of their radar systems. *Aircraft that seemed to be tracked by the Russians didn't even exist: it just appeared to be like that.* The term "ghost aircraft" is a most appropriate one. It's very important to realize the technology Poteat created was in full working order decades ago – and long before the Rendlesham Forest tests occurred.

DECEIVED BY WHAT THEY SAW

Now, think back to the testimony of William Maguire and J.R. Oliver, both of whom were sure they had tracked the movements of huge, unknown craft in U.K. airspace. In Oliver's case it was in 1949, and with regard to Maguire, it happened in 1952. Both men tracked something – or that's how it looked to them. Yet, nothing was ever seen visually. That was precisely the same for the March 26, 1957 incident recorded by staff at Royal Air Force Church Lawford: a UFO, capable of mind-boggling movements was monitored, but it was never ever seen by the human eye. How *could* they see anything? There *was* nothing to see. It was all a strange game. The likelihood is that a version of this technology was utilized to provide the desired result: UFOs in the sky on the nights chaos was breaking out in Rendlersham Forest.

A few more observations: Maguire described the craft he tracked as an "enormous thing with the equivalent mass of a warship." J. R. Oliver wrote that the "UFO" he monitored "offered an echo similar to that of a large passenger or freighter surface vessel." On the matter of huge UFOs that could only be tracked by radar, but never visually, Eugene Poteat said his technology could "...simulate an aircraft of any radar cross section from an invisible stealth plane to one that *made a large blip.*"

I would bet my balls that such very similar large blips were what both Maguire and Oliver were brilliantly deceived by, all those years ago.

Finally, Oliver said his unit handed matters over to "Martlesham radar, with whom we had been in contact." I noted early in this book that Martlesham Heath is approximately just eleven miles from Rendlersham Forest, that British Telecom had a highly secure research facility at Martlesham Heath, Suffolk, and that the whole area was, for decades, smothered in top secret programs dating back to the 1940s, some of them in the field of radar.

When I put all of that together – the Poteat revelations, the "ghost aircraft" phenomenon, and the words of J.R. Oliver and William Maguire – I can only come to one conclusion. In the same way that hallucinogens, holograms and controlled ball lightning were all required, essential parts of this wide-ranging experiment in the trees, so was radar-based technology. It was utilized to make radar operators at nearby bases believe UFOs really were shooting across the sky and those UFOs-that-actually-weren't had been recorded on radar.

Precisely like the military personnel in the forest, the radar operators in the surrounding areas were also the unknowing victims of a series of conjured-up events. It was just yet another way of secretly helping to assist in the burying of a terrible series of experiments on people – and to keep it all hidden under a UFO banner.

REPLY TO
ATTN OF: CD

13 Jan 81

SUBJECT: Unexplained Lights

TO: RAF/CC

1. Early in the morning of 27 Dec 80 (approximately 0300L), two USAF security police patrolmen saw unusual lights outside the back gate at RAF Woodbridge. Thinking an aircraft might have crashed or been forced down, they called for permission to go outside the gate to investigate. The on-duty flight chief responded and allowed three patrolmen to proceed on foot. The individuals reported seeing a strange glowing object in the forest. The object was described as being metallic in appearance and triangular in shape, approximately two to three meters across the base and approximately two meters high. It illuminated the entire forest with a white light. The object itself had a pulsing red light on top and a bank(s) of blue lights underneath. The object was hovering or on legs. As the patrolmen approached the object, it maneuvered through the trees and disappeared. At this time the animals on a nearby farm went into a frenzy. The object was briefly sighted approximately an hour later near the back gate.

2. The next day, three depressions 1 1/2" deep and 7" in diameter were found where the object had been sighted on the ground. The following night (29 Dec 80) the area was checked for radiation. Beta/gamma readings of 0.1 milliroentgens were recorded with peak readings in the three depressions and near the center of the triangle formed by the depressions. A nearby tree had moderate (.05-.07) readings on the side of the tree toward the depressions.

3. Later in the night a red sun-like light was seen through the trees. It moved about and pulsed. At one point it appeared to throw off glowing particles and then broke into five separate white objects and then disappeared. Immediately thereafter, three star-like objects were noticed in the sky, two objects to the north and one to the south, all of which were about 10° off the horizon. The objects moved rapidly in sharp angular movements and displayed red, green and blue lights. The objects to the north appeared to be elliptical through an 8-12 power lens. They then turned to full circles. The objects to the north remained in the sky for an hour or more. The object to the south was visible for two or three hours and beamed down a stream of light from time to time. Numerous individuals, including the undersigned, witnessed the activities in paragraphs 2 and 3.

CHARLES I. HALT, Lt Col, USAF
Deputy Base Commander

Lt. Col. Charles Halt's famous memo on the Rendlesham
Forest affair (United States Air Force).

Survey of Kugelblitz Theories for Electromagnetic Incendiaries (U.S. Army, Edgewood Arsenal).

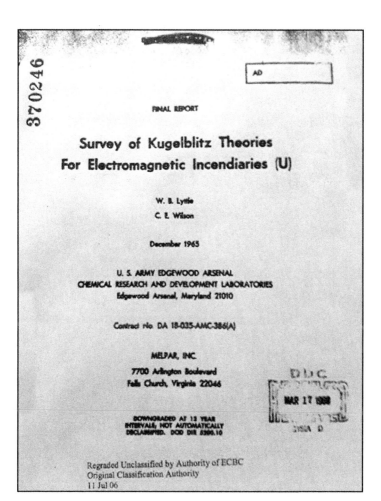

FINAL REPORT

Survey of Kugelblitz Theories
For Electromagnetic Incendiaries (U)

W. B. Lyttle

C. E. Wilson

December 1965

U. S. ARMY EDGEWOOD ARSENAL
CHEMICAL RESEARCH AND DEVELOPMENT LABORATORIES
Edgewood Arsenal, Maryland 21010

Contract No. DA 18-035-AMC-386(A)

MELPAR, INC.

7700 Arlington Boulevard
Falls Church, Virginia 22046

The U.S. military researches ball lightning as a
weapon (U.S. Army, Edgewood Arsenal).

SECURITY

MARKING

The classified or limited status of this report applies
to each page, unless otherwise marked.
Separate page printouts MUST be marked accordingly.

THIS DOCUMENT CONTAINS INFORMATION AFFECTING THE NATIONAL DEFENSE OF
THE UNITED STATES WITHIN THE MEANING OF THE ESPIONAGE LAWS, TITLE 18,
U.S.C., SECTIONS 793 AND 794. THE TRANSMISSION OR THE REVELATION OF
ITS CONTENTS IN ANY MANNER TO AN UNAUTHORIZED PERSON IS PROHIBITED BY
LAW.

NOTICE: When government or other drawings, specifications or other
data are used for any purpose other than in connection with a definitely related government procurement operation, the U. S. Government
thereby incurs no responsibility, nor any obligation whatsoever; and
the fact that the Government may have formulated, furnished, or in any
way supplied the said drawings, specifications, or other data is not
to be regarded by implication or otherwise as in any manner licensing
the holder or any other person or corporation, or conveying any rights
or permission to manufacture, use or sell any patented invention that
may in any way be related thereto.

Ninety-two pages on novel technology
(U.S. Army, Edgewood Arsenal).

Royal Air Force Bentwaters (Nick Redfern).

How it used to be at Bentwaters-Woodbridge (Nick Redfern).

Action at the Edgewood Arsenal (Library of Congress).

U.K. military personnel engaging in secret, hallucinogenic-
based experiments in English woods (U.K. government).

Porton Down as it was in the late 1990s when the UFO links
to the facility were at their height (Matthew Williams).

Ray Boeche, one of the early researchers of the
Rendlesham Forest controversy (Ray Boeche).

Senator Exon, a key figure in the controversy
(United States Senate Historical Office).

United States Senate
WASHINGTON, D.C. 20510

July 9, 1985

Ray W. Boeche, Director

Dear Mr. Boeche:

Thank you for your most recent letter.

As I stated in my last letter to you, while additional information on the subject of the Bentwaters and other unexplained UFO incidents may exist, I can find no evidence of a coverup of UFO incidents by whatever name or reference by any department or agency of the U.S. Government. The executive branch of the government is responsible for the classification of material of national security interest. As it is always possible that this responsibility can be abused, the Congress has the responsibility of oversight. It was this responsibility which I specifically exercised on behalf of you. The Freedom of Information Act further supports this oversight and, when necessary, the judicial system has become involved when the public interest is threatened.

I fully understand that you have pursued this system but are not satisfied with what you have learned. However, after having investigated all possible avenues within the Federal Government, as well as private organizations, I have nothing further to add to what I have previously told you.

I believe that my staff obtained your home address either through a phone conversation with you, or as a result of correspondence with one of the points of contact you provided.

With best wishes.

Cordially,

J. James Exon
United States Senator

Senator J. James "Jim" Exon corresponds
with Ray Boeche (Ray Boeche).

J. JAMES EXON
NEBRASKA

ARMED SERVICES
COMMERCE, SCIENCE, AND
TRANSPORTATION
BUDGET

SENATE HART BUILDING
WASHINGTON, D.C. 20515

FEDERAL BUILDING
LINCOLN, NEBRASKA 68508

FEDERAL BUILDING
OMAHA, NEBRASKA 68102

FEDERAL BUILDING
N. PLATTE, NEBRASKA 69101

United States Senate

WASHINGTON, D.C. 20510

April 2, 1985

Mr. Ray W. Boeche, Dir.
Fortean Research Center
████████████████

Dear Mr. Boeche:

Members of my staff have had the opportunity to read the two books which you loaned to me during our meeting on February 15. As you requested, I am returning them. I have also had the opportunity to listen to the tape.

Frankly, I am not convinced that the incidents you are concerned with did, in fact, occur. Nor have I found any evidence of a cover-up by the government.

However, I have asked the Air Force, National Aeronautics and Space Administration, and the National Academy of Science to address the RAF Bentwaters case. When I have received their replies, I will forward them to you.

If you have any evidence to substantiate the validity of the tape previously provided, I would appreciate your forwarding that information.

With best wishes.

Cordially,

J. James Exon
United States Senator

Enclosures

The UFO researcher and the senator (Ray Boeche).

Graham Birdsall, who broke the story of the planned prison evacuations in December 1980 (Nick Redfern).

The U.K. Ministry of Defense (Nick Redfern).

A mysterious package on the doorstep from
a whistleblower (Nick Redfern).

12

"A THINLY-VEILED, FICTIONAL VERSION OF WHAT HAPPENED"

Over the years and decades, more than a few people who have worked in the worlds of the military, various intelligence communities, and governments have written UFO-based sci-fi novels – mainly, but not exclusively, after they retired from or left the world of officialdom. I mention this because one such writer appeared to have knowledge of at least some of the secrets of Rendlesham Forest, even though he was very careful about what he revealed – and what he held back. He was Ralph Noyes, a man who had a deep interest in two of the primary issues that surface time and time again throughout the book you're reading: UFOs and ball lightning. Before we get to Noyes, however, let's have a look at a few more of the insiders who chose to write fictional stories concerning alien life and extraterrestrial encounters.

In 1948, Bernard Newman wrote a book called *The Flying Saucer*. It told a story of a faked UFO invasion, designed to create a one-world government. Newman was an expert in the field and history of espionage and performed a number of secret operations for U.K. Intelligence during the Second World War.

Dennis Wheatley was a renowned writer of horror novels. He was also a member of the U.K. government's Joint Planning Staff, which was a part of the War Cabinet. Such was the level of respect the government had for Wheatley, he received the rank of Wing Commander – something that made him then the first civilian to have been given such a level. Wheatley's 1952 novel, *Star of Ill-Omen*, is a story of hostile Martians who are determined to take over our world. Imagine something along the lines of an earlier version of the 1996 blockbuster movie, *Independence Day*, and you won't be far off.

"QUESTIONS ABOUT OUR PARTICIPATION IN THIS PROJECT WERE RAISED AT THE HIGHEST LEVEL"

Nineteen-Ninety-Nine was the year in which Nick Pope penned his *Operation Thunder Child* novel. The basic theme was that of a hostile assault on the U.K. By whom? By dangerous extraterrestrials, that's who. When the news surfaced on the Ufological grapevine, it was all but guaranteed some UFO researchers would suggest Pope had written a story based on top secrets he had learned of while working in the MoD. There's *no* evidence there was *any* truth to those suggestions. Although, it must be said Pope was not beyond cultivating an air of intrigue and mystery about himself. He did it very well – and I'm sure that Nick, and his publicists at Simon & Schuster's publishing house, would agree with me. Nevertheless, Pope did make a few comments worth noting.

When the news of *Operation Thunder Child*'s then-looming book surfaced, I asked Nick Pope about his novel – and about the Porton Down angle that appeared in his book, too. I wanted to know what his response was to the fact-vs-fiction scenario of his then-soon-to-be-published book that had the UFO field buzzing. Pope replied: "Even to you, Nick, I can't comment on that. But, let's put it this way: *Operation Thunder Child* is going to be more controversial than *Open Skies, Closed Minds* or *The Uninvited*. And, indeed, the Ministry of Defense may have more of a problem with it. Mainly because it's going to feature real locations, real weapon systems, real tactics, real doctrine and real crisis management techniques. It's going to blend my knowledge and experience of UFOs with my knowledge of crisis management – such as my involvement in the Gulf War, where I worked in the Joint Operations Center."

Pope wasn't done: "Finally, but perhaps most crucially, there are those who, for a number of reasons, I am not able to name. I was helped with this book by a wide range of experts from various different agencies, who supplemented my own knowledge with their insights into the world of politics, science, military doctrine and much else besides."

Pope did, however, point me in the direction of a then-still-serving Ministry of Defense employee, who was willing to make a statement. That man wanted to share with me his thoughts and observations on a BBC show called *Invasion Earth*. It aired in 1998 – one year before *Operation Thunder Child* was released. In *Invasion Earth*, Porton Down played a significant role. I'll now share with you the words of the MoD source:

"It's extremely strange that on the one hand the MoD is publicly so dismissive about UFOs; and yet on the other they bent over backwards to provide assistance to a TV company producing a science-fiction drama which starts with the Royal Air Force shooting down a UFO. Normally, the Ministry of Defense only helps film and TV companies where it believes that significant benefits will fall to the MoD in terms of recruiting, training or public relations. This was the case, for example, with our participation in the James Bond film, *Tomorrow Never Dies*. What, one wonders, did the MoD think it had to gain from helping to perpetuate a view that the Royal Air Force were virtually at war with extra-terrestrials? Questions about our participation in this project were raised at the highest level within the Ministry of Defense."

HOW TO MISLEAD AND DECEIVE

The year 2000 was when Georgina Bruni's important discoveries about Porton Down and Rendlesham Forest appeared publicly - in her book *You Can't tell the People*. I know from speaking to Georgina on many occasions, though, she had been working on her book for several years prior to its publication. Did someone in government (who knew Georgina's revelations would ultimately surface, even if it was still a couple of years down the line) decide that certain action had to be done to try and diffuse what Georgina had unearthed about the Rendlesham Forest-Porton Down connection? Was a plan initiated to encourage the idea, via the media and the world of on-screen entertainment, that there were real ties between Porton Down and aliens?

That would have been much more preferable than having an enterprising journalist discover the *real* story of UFOs and Porton Down was actually driven by classified tests designed to determine just how much fucking the human mind could take. Or, in some cases, *couldn't*. The people behind the operations may have come up with something very much like a scenario I have conjured up: "If we can't hide the truth of Porton Down's secret experiments in Rendlesham Forest, and we can't stop the publication of Georgina Bruni's book, then let's swamp and distort the truth with incredible tales, whistleblowers, TV shows, and novels."

And all with connections to extraterrestrial entities at Porton Down. A dark truth is very often hidden via a well thought out diversion. And it doesn't get much darker than this one.

We need to take a further look at the writing of Nick Pope – partly because in *Operation Thunder Child* Pope has aliens taken to none other than Porton Down. Was this a case of Pope trying to tell people there really was a Porton Down connection to the UFO phenomenon? Or, was it a case of Pope hoping people would think just that, as a means to help boost his book sales? I vividly recall discussing this specific issue with the staff of *UFO Magazine* in late 2000. Most felt that Pope was an astute opportunist and nothing more. A few suggested Pope used his knowledge learned at the MoD and weaved genuine, sensitive, government secrets into *Operation Thunder Child*. Pope returned to non-fiction writing in 2015, with his book *Encounter in Rendlesham Forest*. Claims of Porton Down connections to the Rendlesham case appear in the pages of the 2015 Pope-Penniston-Burroughs book.

The career of a man named Ralph Noyes comes into play, too. His strange foray into the world of science fiction took off with a novel titled *A Secret Property*. A careful reading of Noyes' book suggests he knew something of what happened in Rendlesham Forest at Christmas 1980 – and in specific relation to those top secret experiments.

"HE HAS BECOME INCREASINGLY INTERESTED IN THIS SUBJECT"

The publishers of Noyes' novel – Quartet Books, Ltd. – provided their readers with the following background on their author: "Ralph Noyes was born in the tropics and spent most of his childhood in the West Indies. He served in the RAF from 1940 to 1946 and was commissioned as aircrew, engaging in active service in North Africa and the Far East. He entered the civil service in 1949 and served in the Air Ministry and subsequently the unified Ministry of Defense. In 1977 he retired early from the civil service to take up a writing career, leaving in the grade of under Secretary of State. He has since published several pieces of shorter fiction, most of them on speculative themes."

The publishers added: "For nearly four years, until late 1972, Ralph Noyes headed a division in the central staffs of the Ministry of Defense which brought him in touch with the UFO problem. Since his retirement he has become increasingly interested in this subject, among others which lie on the fringes of present understanding. He sees speculative fiction as the ideal mode for grappling with these unusual areas of experience. But *A Secret Property* is not only fiction but also 'faction'–at least to the extent of drawing on Ralph Noyes's lengthy background in the Royal Air Force and the Ministry of Defense."

There's more to it all than that, I should note.

HOW MUCH WAS FACT AND HOW MUCH WAS FICTION?

A Secret Property is a thinly veiled, fictional version of what happened at Rendlesham Forest. Consider the following: in Noyes' story we have a Colonel Hoyt, a military base called Bentbridge, and mysterious action deep in the woods. And, Noyes had the absolute gall to deny his story was a *roman-à-clef.* The *Grammarist* says: "A *roman-à-clef* is a novel which depicts real-world people and events, with fictional names. Usually, details concerning the people and events are changed in minor ways in order to sustain the pretense of fiction. The amount of fictionalization in a *roman-à-clef* can vary widely."

In Noyes' case, the amount was huge.

Most important of all, it is not the matter of how much data and material Noyes chose to fictionalize in *A Secret Property*. Rather, it's the *theme* of Noyes' story that is so important and relevant to us – more than thirty-five years after his book was published. In her 1991 book *From Out of the Blue*, Jenny Randles said of Noyes' story that it involved a technology that "produces etheric visions of aliens and spaceships" and can "effect the real world in various hazardous ways."

In her third book on the subject of Rendlesham - *UFO Crash Landing?* - Randles got right to the heart of the matter, pointing out something that has been largely overlooked by so many in Ufology. Jenny said that Noyes' scenario in *A Secret Property* brought together "sophisticated computer-controlled technology with the power within human consciousness and the natural forces of the Earth itself. Blending both mind and electronics together, it endeavored to forge a powerful 'psychic' weapon."

Just about everything Noyes wrote about in his 1985 novel - and that Randles discussed in relation to Noyes - smacks of classified operations, visionary experiences, and strange technology; all of which are at the heart of the overall "secret experiment" scenario that dominates *The Rendlesham Forest UFO Conspiracy*. Randles may not have realized how close she came to penetrating the truth of the matter. I would say she was right on the cusp of one of the most important parts of this overall story. Unfortunately, yet predictably, in the 1990s mainstream Ufology was still way too excited – years after Rendlesham occurred – by tales of aliens and extraterrestrial spaceships. Much of that was prompted by the influence that the hugely popular show *The X-File*s had on the U.K.'s Ufology.

Noyes knew something of what happened in the woods – or, at the very least, he *had his suspicions* about the genuine scenario. Perhaps, those suspicions came via government sources – possibly, even, from retired colleagues from the MoD, who may have provided a few snippets of information and strategically-placed clues. In all probability, though, Noyes *never* knew the full story, but learned enough of it to allow him to blend the shocking truth into a readable page-turner. Noyes did us all a service by trying to get the truth of Rendlesham into the open, and without causing himself problems with his old employers at the Ministry of Defense. He was, after all, on a government pension, something that would certainly have led him to tread very carefully.

"THE CASE CAN HARDLY BE WITHOUT DEFENSE SIGNIFICANCE"

Ralph Noyes was interviewed by Andy Roberts and Dr. David Clarke, who have both taken an interest in the Rendlesham case. Noyes told the pair: "In the several capacities which brought me into touch with UFO reports during my 28 years in the MoD, I encountered several reports, particularly those from military establishments, which indicated 'high strangeness.' I, and military colleagues, had little doubt something had taken place for which we had no explanation."

On the matter of what happened in those woods – or what didn't happen, depending where you're coming from – Noyes offered the following to Clarke and Roberts: "There is no doubt at all that the MoD played a thoroughly dishonest game over the Rendlesham affair...The case itself is complex. I have given my own views about it - essentially that Halt and several others came face to face with a striking manifestation of the 'UFO phenomenon' whatever that may be, in the December of 1980."

Noyes also made this highly valid statement: "Unless Lt. Col. Halt was out of his mind, there is clear evidence in his report that British airspace and territory were intruded upon by an unidentified vehicle on two occasions in late December 1980 and that no authority was able to prevent this. If, on the other hand, Halt's report cannot be believed, there is equally clear evidence of a serious misjudgment of events by USAF personnel at an important base in British territory. Either way, the case can hardly be without defense significance."

RECOLLECTIONS OF RALPH

Dennis Stacy, with Patrick Huyghe, runs Anomalist Books – and they do a great job of publishing books on all manner of paranormal phenomena. Stacy had the good fortune to meet Ralph Noyes many years ago. Stacy would come to learn Noyes had an interest in ball lighting. Stacy recalls his times spent with Noyes:

"I first came into contact with Noyes during the late 1980s, when he submitted an article (if memory serves) about ball lightning to the *MUFON UFO Journal,* of which I was then editor. I accepted it, a correspondence followed, and so did a handful of subsequent articles on the newest mystery of the time - crop circles…"

Stacy tells of the time he visited Noyes in his, Noyes', home in London, England: "Among the ashtrays was a computer he was learning. His fingers were never far from a cigarette and neither were mine in those days. As quickly became evident, we both shared a love of the pulped grape as well, a dark burgundy, preferably. We puffed and sipped, sipped and puffed, and of course conversed. What were these miraculous new crop circles? Did they bear an intimate relation to ball lightning and / or UFOs? Fine and well; now, what would either of *those* be?"

Tactful and fairly tight-lipped to the very end, Noyes – I predict - will one day be seen as a key figure in the unravelling and exposing of the subterfuge, denial and camouflage that surrounds the many and varied things that occurred in Rendesham Forest.

13

"STILL BARELY UNDERSTOOD"

May 2006 was the date on which a remarkable revelation surfaced. It added yet further weight to the fact that the Ministry of Defense has a remarkable interest in ball lightning and plasmas – and using them as weapons. It was a revelation that made UFO researchers all across the world sit up and listen and look. For a number of years, it was disclosed, the U.K.'s Ministry of Defense had been secretly working on a UFO program. I must make it clear it wasn't the kind of project that had dead aliens and crashed UFOs – as per Roswell – at its heart. Nevertheless, the disclosure was stunning all the same. Between 1996 – when the operation began – and February 2000, when the project was completed, the MoD had been carefully and quietly investigating the UFO puzzle. The program's official title was *Unidentified Aerial Phenomena in the UK Air Defense Region*. Unofficially, it went by the far less lengthy name of *Project Condign*.

It was due to the U.K.'s Freedom of Information Act the Report surfaced – and with thanks to the investigations of UFO researchers Dr. David Clarke and Gary Anthony. The pair worked hard to try and get the report released. That work eventually paid off. In spades, no less. The 465-pages-long report was a fascinating one. Despite the fact the MoD always maintained it had very little interest in UFOs, the sheer length and depth of the report showed this was, at the very least, a misunderstanding. Or, at the other extreme, an outright lie. A great deal of focus was placed on the author of the report. His name remained hidden behind closed doors for quite a few years. But, nothing stays hidden forever. The elderly man was outed as a Dr. Ron Haddow.

In 2006, Haddow wrote an adventure-driven novel titled *No Weapon Forged*. It was reviewed in that same year by John Nicholls, who was writing for *Testimony Magazine*. In part, Nicholls noted Haddow "spent the early part of his life in the Royal Air Force, both in flying and in testing the first airborne digital equipment to enter RAF service. His work then changed to teaching radar, electronic warfare, air defense and guided weapons, with special reference to Middle East warfare." Nicholls continued that Haddow, "continued in research and design of equipment, and later became a Senior Advisor to a NATO Industrial Advisory Group work on future defenses…"

That's quite a body of work.

"PLASMA FORMATIONS, WHICH HAVE POTENTIAL APPLICATIONS TO NOVEL WEAPON TECHNOLOGY"

For years, the U.K. UFO research community sought to find out who it was that wrote *Project Condign*. A good friend of mine, Irene Bott, almost got to the heart of the mystery in the late 1990s. From 1996 to 2000, Irene ran the U.K.-based *Staffordshire UFO Group*. On one particular day while I was hanging out at Irene's then-home, she put a call in to the MoD. The purpose was to inquire about a UFO incident she was looking into. For reasons that still remain fully unclear to this day, Irene was transferred by the MoD operator who answered her call not to the MoD's

"UFO desk" that Nick Pope previously ran, but to none other than Ron Haddow.

Documentation now in the public domain shows that Haddow and his colleagues were deeply concerned by this spectacular error. That Haddow actually engaged Irene in conversation hardly impressed the Ministry of Defense, as the now-declassified documents on the Haddow-Bott conversation show. In a few minutes of online handiwork, and with Haddow's name in-hand, Irene and I had Haddow's home address and his landline number. By all accounts, the whole thing caused a fair degree of concern within the MoD. And for Haddow, too.

It has to be said that when word of the report got out of the *Condign Report*, more than a few UFO investigators thought the MoD was getting ready to admit to the possibility aliens were really visiting us. I know, because I spoke with more than a few of those same investigators. They were sure that "UFO Disclosure" was coming. It did *not* arrive. The MoD and Haddow were far more interested by something distinctly different. Namely: *plasmas and ball lighting. And their potential novel uses for the military purposes.*

I wrote an article on all of this for *Fortean Times* shortly after the story surfaced. A portion of it states: "Inevitably, many UFO investigators claimed that the MoD's report was merely a ruse to hide its secret knowledge of alien encounters, crashed UFOs, and high-level *X-Files*-type conspiracies. And although the Government firmly denied such claims, the report did reveal a number of significant conclusions of a genuinely intriguing nature. The atmospheric plasmas which were believed to be the cause of so many UFO reports were 'still barely understood,' said the MoD; and the magnetic and electric fields that emanated from plasmas could adversely affect the human nervous system. And that was not all. Clarke and Anthony revealed that 'Volume 3 of the report refers to research and studies carried out in a number of foreign nations into UAPs [Unidentified Aerial Phenomena], atmospheric plasmas, and their potential military applications."'

One of the documents, of December 4, 2000, and given the heading of *Unidentified Aerial Phenomena (UAP) - DI55 Report,* included the following words: "DG(R&T) [Director-General, Research & Technology] will be interested in those phenomena associated with *plasma formations, which have potential applications to novel weapon technology* [italics mine]."

"PLASMA RELATED FIELDS AND THE TEMPORAL LOBES IN THE BRAIN"

Further information came to fruition thanks to James Randerson, a journalist with the *Guardian* newspaper. In an article titled "Could we have hitched a ride on UFOs?" he wrote: "According to a former MoD intelligence analyst who asked not be named, the MoD was paranoid in the late 1980s that the Soviet Union had developed technology that went beyond western knowledge of physics. 'For many years we were very concerned that in some areas the Russians had a handle on physics that we hadn't at all. We just basically didn't know the basics they were working from,' he said. 'We did encourage our scientists not to think that we in the west knew everything there was to be known.'"

Nick Pope had his say, too: "One of the areas that will be most contentious relates to what the report refers to as 'plasma related fields.' Electrically-charged atmospheric plasmas are credited with having given rise to some of the reports of vast triangular-shaped craft, *while the interaction of such plasma fields with the temporal lobes in the brain is cited as another reason why people might feel they were having a strange experience* [italics mine]."

14

"SOMETHING BEING TESTED IN THE AREA"

There is a little-known phenomenon that deserves coverage in this book. It concerns several other U.K.-based operations that can be viewed as near-identical to the Rendlesham Forest incidents. All of these additional encounters involved military personnel and were clearly staged. That's right: Rendlesham was not a stand-alone incident. The mind-manipulators appear to have been engaged in their incredibly alternative, and duplicity-driven, operations for a very long time – and all under extraterrestrial banners. So far as things can be determined right now, matters began in the early 1960s. Interestingly, that was when Porton Down got highly pro-active, in terms of using military personnel for their experiments on the human mind. Not only that, these experiments were still being orchestrated and executed up to - at the very least - the 1990s.

"A GLOBE-LIKE DAZZLING BALL"

We'll begin with the experience of Paul Greensill. His confrontation of the mystifying type happened back in 1962. He retired from the British Army in August of that year, after having served with 9 Parachute Squadron, Royal Engineers. With a successful military career behind him, Greensill then enlisted in the Army Reserve. The Ministry of Defense provides background: "The Army Reserve is the largest of the Reserve Forces. The Army Reserve provides support to the Regular Army at home and overseas, and throughout its history almost every major operation has seen reservists operate alongside their Regular counterparts. Army Reserve Soldiers come from all walks of life and work part-time as soldiers for the British Army alongside full-time Regular soldiers."

It was in August 1963 when Greensill and his comrades were taking part in a training-based military operation not too far from Ripon, Yorkshire, England. It was an exercise comprised of around forty personnel and began shortly before midnight. Suddenly, *a globe-like, dazzling ball of light* - directed ball lightning, most likely – shot across the skies and stopped over the amazed troops at a height of no more than about eighty or ninety feet. It hung silently in the sky for several minutes, after which it accelerated away at a fast speed. It then briefly returned, after which it yet again soared away into the starlit night. No official report was made, said Greensill. But, just about everyone was excitedly talking about the events the following day – which is not at all surprising. Despite the lack of official paperwork, Greensill said that the higher-ups were keen to see what the regular troops thought of it all.

Today, interestingly, 9 Parachute Squadron RE is stationed at Rock Barracks at... *Woodbridge, Suffolk*. What goes around certainly comes around, it would seem. With that case addressed, here's another for you.

"A CIRCULAR, SILVERY THING"

Approximately two years before the dense trees of Rendlesham Forest were lit up and lives were forever changed, something similar occurred on the U.K.'s expansive and wild Yorkshire Moors. In this case, however, the witnesses were not American military personnel, but two Englishmen: Mike Perrin and "Titch" Carvell. At the time, both men were with the British Army's Royal Armored Corps. As the name of the RAC suggests, its role is to provide the armor capability of the Army, such as tanks. Perrin and Carvell were taking part in a military exercise on the moors when a decidedly strange intruder suddenly appeared on the scene – and right at the time the pair, in their *Land Rover*, was carefully negotiating a winding stretch of road.

Suddenly, a circular, silvery thing appeared out of nowhere and hung in the air at a precarious level and at a distance of around 140-150 feet. Even at that distance they could hear a loud, "strange buzzing" coming from the object. Suddenly, the engine of the *Land Rover* died and the vehicle coasted to a stop. That was most assuredly not a good thing. In fact, it was a decidedly ominous thing.

Perrin said: "It was about the size of five *Land Rovers* and had portholes. Lights inside were flashing red and white. I tried to start our vehicle, but the engine was totally dead. We watched the UFO for five minutes, then it shot off and all the power returned to our engine. It's Army policy to dismiss UFO reports, but when we went back to the area next morning with a sergeant, we found a large circle of burnt grass where the object had hovered." The event was over.

A staged event for the "benefit" of Perrin and Carvell? I'd say "Yes."

"WHEN THIS THING CAME ALONG, IT WAS
ACTUALLY A BALL OF LIGHT"

The following incident, which is almost identical to the collective Rendlesham Forest events, occurred in the early 1990s at yet *another* military base in Suffolk, England. On this occasion it was RAF Lakenheath. As *Militarybases.com* state of the base: "Royal Air Force Lakenheath is a RAF military base that is run and operated by the U.S. Air Force. It exclusively hosts American troops. It is located in Suffolk, in the eastern part of the United Kingdom... The installation is a co-base run by the Americans under the British regulations and laws...It was activated on site in 1952 and represents one of the longest lasting units in the Air Force, serving in the area for almost 60 years. The wing counts almost 8000 individuals. About 2000 of them are British civilians and family members, while almost 6000 are active military troops."

The original source of the story was a UFO researcher named Roy Wilkinson. He shared it, in the late-1990s, with Matthew Williams. The latter is someone who, for a number of years, was a Criminal Investigator with Her Majesty's Customs and Excise agency. Today, it is called HM Revenue and Customs. Williams told me that it was late one night, during the course of military operations in Suffolk woods, when something very strange happened. Over to Williams: "*A report came through that on one particular night those on maneuvers should expect to see something being tested in the area; and when the testing was taking place, they were to ignore it: pretend it's not there and carry as normal.* [Italics mine]."

"THOSE SENIOR OFFICERS WANTED TO KNOW WHAT THE WITNESSES THOUGHT OF THE INCIDENT"

Quite understandably, as Williams says: "They found this a bit hard to do, because when this thing came along, *it was actually a ball of light* [italics mine] and was too small to be manned – so it had to be a remote drone of some kind, they thought. But, it was pure light, no mechanics, no rockets, no noise, which makes me think it wasn't a drone. And this thing moved silently above the area where they were on maneuvers – off the base and in the woods." Indeed, as *Military.com* note: "Lakenheath is located in Forest Heath District of Suffolk County in East Anglia, England."

Back to Williams: "Then, the light increased in intensity and illuminated the whole area like a flare would. Everyone stopped what they were doing, and just broke their orders. They watched this thing for a minute or so, and then it diminished in size and went off at a high speed into the distance. Everyone was talking about this and, really, it unnerved them to a certain degree. The whole evening's events were then called off, because everything was in such a state of disarray. If the military experimented with things which could be perceived to be UFOs, i.e., balls of light, then – because of their knowledge that the event was going to happen – they would have to have those UFOs stored somewhere near."

Both tellingly and suspiciously, the very next day, several of the personnel involved were extensively questioned by senior officers. Those senior officers wanted to know what the witnesses thought of the incident: did they believe the statement something had been "tested" in the skies over Suffolk? Or did they distrust their senior officers, and think it was really a UFO that was encountered? Could it have been an alien spacecraft? Did anyone have strange dreams after returning to their base and falling asleep after dawn?

What was it that caused them to go against their orders? Was the whole thing too fantastic and panic-inducing to prevent the men from operating in the ways expected of the military? These were fascinating questions. They were also questions that suggested the senior officers in charge of the operation were very keen to see what the effects were on the men who were exposed to the strange phenomenon.

"IN THE WRONG PLACE AND WRONG TIME"

With a fair degree of hindsight, we can safely say that the Lakenheath incident was a perfectly orchestrated operation designed to see just how far and wide the human mind could be tampered with – and using unwitting military personnel as the targeted individuals. It may be of significance that all of those who were chosen to take part in the operation, and who saw the ball of light, were the youngest and the newest to be assigned to the base. You'll now see why the age issue is an important part of the Lakenheath story.

The parallels between the Lakenheath incident in the early 1990s and the far more well-known and legendary incident in Rendlesham Forest are remarkable. In both cases, the locations were woodland. Both events occurred late at night. There were multiple witnesses. The reference to a "ball of light" seen near Lakenheath very much echoes what was seen by Colonel Halt and his team in Rendlesham Forest in December 1980. Both bases had sizeable numbers of U.S. personnel in residency. Lakenheath still does. The official website of RAF Lakenheath notes: "Royal Air Force Lakenheath, United Kingdom, is located 70 miles northeast of London and 25 miles northeast of Cambridge. The Liberty Wing consists of more than 4,500 active-duty military members, over 1,000 British and U.S. civilians and includes a geographically-separated unit at nearby RAF Feltwell. RAF Lakenheath is the largest U.S. Air Force-operated base in England and the only U.S. Air Forces in Europe (USAFE) F-15 fighter wing."

And, we know that many of the Rendlesham victims were still very young when the events kicked off, just like those who were secretly brought in for the Lakenheath experiment. Very much the same can be said for the experience of Paul Greensill, and that of Mike Perrin and "Titch" Carvell: all three happened to be "conveniently" in the right place and at the right time, undergoing military operations and exercises, and primed to see something that most of us never get to encounter.

To me, this suggests secret manipulation to an astonishing degree. Jenny Randles said: "I have found two fascinating cases that may well tie in with this theory." One occurred at the Dhekelia Station in Cyprus which is "situated within the Eastern Sovereign Base Area, one of two British Sovereign Base Areas in Cyprus, enshrined in the Treaty of Establishment between the U.K. and the Republic of Cyprus in 1960." The other was a Spanish military installation: Talvera La Real Air Base. In the former case, said Jenny, a "glowing form" was seen. In the other, a "monstrous alien" was encountered.

"IF THEY CAN GET IN HERE, THEY CAN GET IN ANYWHERE"

I have a similar case to those referred to by Jenny Randles, and which also occurred in a sensitive installation. This one comes from Hillary Gough, of the town of Farnborough, Hampshire, England. The date was early 1974, and the setting, the Marconi Space and Defense Systemes, Ltd., at Frimley, England. At the time, Gough was employed as a draughtswoman in the Central Services branch – having previously served an apprenticeship in a division of the British Royal Navy – which ensured she had access to much of the establishment.

"Something very serious has happened, hasn't it?" she inquired. "Yes," was the quiet response. "We've had a break-in. I can't say anymore." Over the course of several weeks, however, further pieces of the puzzle fell into place. It transpired that the break-in was far more than simply an unauthorized entry. What occurred was nothing short of the penetration of a highly sensitive facility by what some of the staff suspected was an extraterrestrial creature.

I was cautiously advised the incident had occurred late at night, and the one witness was a security guard who had been patrolling the building as part of his routine duty. While walking along a corridor, the guard was startled by a dazzling blue light that emanated from one particular room. But this was no ordinary room: it was a storage facility for top secret documentation generated by Marconi as part of its work on behalf of the British Government and the Ministry of Defense, much of which was related to classified, radar-based programs.

Realizing that no one – at all – should have been in the area at that time of night, the guard burst into the room, only to be confronted by a shocking sight. There, literally sifting through pages and pages of top-secret files was a gray-skinned humanoid – but decidedly non-human – creature which quickly dematerialized before the shocked guard's eyes. Although severely traumatized by the event, he was able to provide a brief description of the being to his superiors and noted that the blue light emanated from a helmet encompassed the head of the entity.

By the following morning the guard had suffered a near-complete nervous collapse and was taken away, under a military guard, to an unspecified hospital for intensive therapy. He was not seen at the Frimley facility again. Some weeks later, Hillary Gough had occasion to overhear snippets of a conversation that occurred in the office of her boss.

I have been advised that the following is a close approximation of the relevant section of the conversation between the two: "We have no way of keeping these beings out; we just don't know what to do next. If they can get in here, they can get in anywhere."

Full-on believers in alien encounters will likely take the story to be exactly what it appears to have been - an encounter of a very traumatic type that involved an extraterrestrial and a terrified man. I'm far more skeptical, however. On this matter, I'll close with the words of Jenny Randles, as they relate to the two similar cases she investigated: "In each case the humanoid figure that was seen glowed with a phosphorous-like energy in vivid colors that are not unlike the oranges and greens *that accompany laser-projected holograms* [Italics mine]."

"INTERNATIONAL ANTI-NUCLEAR PROTEST"

RAF Greenham Common is a now-shutdown U.K. military base that also had a high degree of controversy attached to it. As for the facility and its history, there is this: "Royal Air Force Greenham Common or RAF Greenham Common is a former Royal Air Force station in Berkshire, England. The airfield was southeast of Newbury, Berkshire, about 55 miles (89 km) west of London. Opened in 1942, it was used by both the Royal Air Force and United States Army Air Forces during the Second World War and the United States Air Force during the Cold War, also as a base for nuclear weapons. After the Cold War ended, it was closed in September 1992."

Historic England notes of the base: "The first cruise missiles were delivered in November 1983 and by 1986 there were 96 missiles and five spares made up into six mobile cruise missile flights housed at GAMA [the Ground launched Cruise Missile Alert and Maintenance Area]…Peace camps were established around the base perimeter fence and the Greenham women, in opposition to the deployment of cruise missiles, used non-violent protest to bring the nuclear capability of Greenham Common airbase and the campaign for nuclear disarmament to the attention of the world. It is for this reason that Greenham Common is a name which is internationally famous; a site which is symbolic of international anti-nuclear protest."

TURNING WEAPONS ON U.K. CITIZENS

It was in the 1980s that Greenham Common became almost notorious in the U.K. There was a reason for that: when the controversy surrounding the nuclear weapons held at the base was at its height, a large group of women decided to protest outside of the base, and very clear to the fences. They received a huge amount of coverage from the nation's media. They received something else too: severe ill-health. While demonstrating outside, the women soon began to experience memory loss, severe headaches, overwhelming panic, and depression. Rumors got around the military was secretly using low- and high-frequency weapons, all aimed at the women – the goal being to try and get them to leave the base and move on. They did not.

The media was soon onto this portion of the story too. The *Guardian* newspaper splashed an article on the story in its pages in 1986. Its title: "Peace Women Fear Electronic Zapping at Base." In the article, it was said the base security personnel had in their possession "an intruder detection system called BISS, Base Installation Security System, which operates on a sufficiently high frequency to bounce radar waves off a human body moving in the vicinity of a perimeter fence."

"THE WOMEN EXPERIENCED SYMPTOMS
CHARACTERISTIC OF ELF IRRADIATION"

Jim Keith, in *Mind Control and UFOs*, chased down this story, too: "A probable instance of the use of ELF weapons on civilians took place in January of 1985, when women protesting nuclear weapons at the U.S. Air Force Base at Greenham Common in England began experiencing strange physical symptoms, coincident with the changing of the security system at the base from primarily human to electronic. Guards patrolling the base's perimeter were reduced in number, and antennae were installed at intervals. The women experienced symptoms characteristic of ELF irradiation, including headaches, earaches, pressure behind the eyes, bleeding from nose and gums, fatigue, the hearing of clicks and buzzes, and heart palpitations. Electronic testing performed by a Canadian scientist and a British electronics activist group confirmed distinct areas of electromagnetic activity around the women's camps."

The base is long gone now: "On 11 September 1992, USAF returned RAF Greenham Common to the Ministry of Defense. In February 1993, the Greenham Common air base was declared surplus to requirements by the Secretary of State for Defense and the airfield was put up for sale. The Greenham Common Trust was formed in 1997 to run the technical side of the base which became a business park. The airfield side was opened to the public in 2000."

What we have here, then, are top secret experiments undertaken at a U.K.-based Royal Air Force base in the 1980s, and at which secret technologies and weaponry were used to affect minds and nervous-systems and with one goal: overwhelming destabilization.

15

"SEE TO IT THAT THESE ARE BURIED"

By this time, some of you may be wondering just how much of the UFO phenomenon is real, and how much is the top secret work of scientists working for the Department of Defense, the Pentagon, and Porton Down's scientists. And who knows how many other labs and agencies, too? Keeping in mind what we've been exposed to so far, it's a valid and logical question to ask. It may crush your belief-systems, but the grim fact is that such UFO-linked manipulation of the public and of unwitting military personnel didn't begin with Rendlesham. That was certainly the pinnacle of it all (as far as we know), but it has been going on since the very early days of Ufology. Much of it occurred in the United States – and with two particularly notorious incidents having occurred in the 1950s: one in France and the other in Brazil.

It's most important I address those earlier French and American cases that are about to cross your path. As to why, it's for this reason: they demonstrate how drugs, hallucinogens, and faked and staged events of a Rendlesham Forest type have been run on far more occasions than you might expect. We'll begin with a story of horrendous proportions – which, as you'll see, is an ideal and appropriate description for what's coming now.

FROM CHAOS TO CRAZED

If you think that entire groups of people cannot be rendered into altered states of perception – and at the manipulative hands and minds of intelligence agencies – you would be acutely wrong. Prepare yourself for the shocking facts concerning a terrible and terrifying saga that went down in a small town in France in the early 1950s. Its name: Pont-Saint-Esprit. It's a small locale, the origins of which date back centuries and that, today, only has a population of around 11,000. As for the horrific things that happened on August 15, 1951, they were almost unbelievable. Matters started just like any other day in the town. By the end of the day, however, things were very different.

What you are about to read might seem like the plotline of an apocalypse-type, big-bucks movie. It is not. The truth is far more frightening than anything Hollywood ever concocted. It was no time at all before many of the residents began to have intense hallucinations of all manner of strange creatures and monsters in their midst. Some of them even began to act like crazed beasts. The cause of the event – or, rather, of the *claimed* cause – was the ingestion of a fungus called ergot, and that had reportedly got into the town's food supply.

Ergot, a fungal disease of various cereals, can have a mind-blowing effect on a person when it invades the human body. And, so we are told, that is exactly what happened to the people of Pont-Saint-Esprit. In her 2006 book, *Hunting the American Werewolf*, Linda Godfrey says of this notoriously weird story that "ergot is now widely regarded as a possible cause of the bestial madness. According to this theory, it was not demonic influence but the ingestion of *Claviceps purpurea* (which contains a compound similar to LSD), which led to the demented behavior and thus, executions, of many alleged witches, werewolves, and vampires."

By the end of the day, more than *250 people* in town were affected – and dangerously so, too. By the next day, four people were dead and dozens more were in asylums. The survivors were held within the walls of the imposing buildings for the safety of not just the affected, but also for the safety of the doctors and nurses who were treating them.

A SECRET EXPERIMENT GETS OUT OF CONTROL

It's now time to look at the startling, *real* answer for what happened at Point-Saint-Esprit back in 1951. In the years that have passed since the events occurred, an ever-growing body of data has surfaced, all of which makes a strong case for the theory that the poor people of the town were *deliberately* targeted – primarily to see how hallucinogens can affect the human mind. Those behind the experiment quickly found out.

Investigative author H. P. Albarelli, Jr., is the author of *A Terrible Mistake*. It's a book that tells the shocking story – and death - of a man named Frank Olson. At the time the events in France were erupting, Olson was employed as a chemist at the U.S. Army's Special Operations Division. For a while, that is. Olson lost his life on November 28, 1953: he was pushed, or he jumped, from the 10th floor of the Manhattan's Hotel Statler (today, the Hotel Pennsylvania). It has to be said Albarelli makes a very strong case that Olson *did not* commit suicide, but was thrown out of the window of the hotel – because Olson was on the verge of revealing to the media that behind the scenes in the labs of the CIA and the Army, weird experiments were afoot to manipulate the mind.

It's most intriguing to note Frank Olson was in France in both 1950 and 1951 – where he met with French intelligence personnel who were very interested in the growing realm of mind-control. Thanks to the relentless research of Albarelli – and the terms of the Freedom of Information Act - we now know Olson's name appears in once-classified CIA files that are related to Pont-Saint-Esprit. One such document reads as follows: "Re: Pont-Saint-Esprit and F. Olson files. SO Span / France Operation file, including Olson. Intel files. Hand carry to Berlin – tell him to see to it that these are buried."

It's very clear this particular memo was written in a form that only those in the know, within the CIA, would understand the precise nature of what was being discussed. That certain "files" were planned on being "buried" by agency personnel, and that this all had a connection to Frank Olson and Pont-Saint-Esprit, strongly suggests that what happened in France in 1951 was a ruthless, deliberate test on the locals and with the help of the CIA.

It's important to pay careful attention to what was going on in the United States in roughly the same time - and all in relation to top secret plans designed to freak out minds and have people think they were seeing alien-based phenomena when, really, they were not.

DEMYSTIFYING ONE OF UFOLOGY'S
MOST FAMOUS ENCOUNTERS

Flatwoods, West Virginia, is situated in Braxton County and is a town of less than three hundred people. It dates back to the latter part of the 19th century and makes for a pleasant visit. The landscape is wooded and hilly, and provides a captivating picture. For such a tiny town, though, Flatwoods has become famous: it was the location of one of the most legendary of all

UFO encounters of the 1950s. September 12, 1952 was the night on which something bizarre, out of this world, and beastly paid Flatwoods a menacing visit that they have never forgotten, decades on. Or, those same townsfolk were the manipulated targets of a very strange experiment.

The expert on the story is Frank C. Feschino, Jr. His extensive research into the case led him to write an excellent book on the subject: *The Braxton County Monster*. He says that on the night when the town was destined to forever become famous, a strange, bright object fell from the sky in a hilly area in town. Feschino expands: "A group of schoolboys saw the object maneuver across the sky and seemingly fall to Earth." He asks: "Was it a meteor, plane or anything they could explain? The boys and two adults headed off to look for the object. Soon a twelve-foot tall being from the downed craft terrified these innocent people. This being became known as 'The Flatwoods Monster,' or 'The Braxton County Monster.'"

History was made – and in rapid time: UFO investigators were practically frothing at their mouths. And the media was quickly onto the story. But did the incident really have anything to do with aliens? Many might say, "Yes!" And firmly and decisively so, too. But, what if – and *just like* the Rendlesham incidents – the Flatwoods Monster was not evidence of an extraterrestrial visitation at all? What if the monster of Flatwoods was the creation of the U.S. Air Force, playing games with the local population, and all as a means to see how the minds of far more than a few people could be significantly dabbled with?

"INGENIOUS - AND VERY LARGE
SCALE - ILLUSION SYSTEMS"

To understand the true nature and origin of the Flatwoods Monster, we are required to take a trip back to the latter stages of the Second World War – to the mountains of Italy, specifically. And, we have a man named Jasper Maskelyne to thank for shedding light on what would materialize in West Virginia woods in 1952. You may wonder, who, exactly, was Maskelyne? The answer comes from the *Magic Tricks* website: "Jasper Maskelyne, grandson of John Nevil Maskelyne, was an invaluable resource to his native Britain during World War II. Maskelyne became an integral part of a special unit focused on the action along the Suez Canal. With his great knowledge of illusion, Maskelyne was able to devise ingenious - and very large scale - illusion systems that virtually made tanks invisible from the air, hid whole buildings full of ammunition and supplies, and even made an entire city vanish and reappear several miles away."

Maskelyne didn't possess magical, supernatural powers: he was just a brilliant magician; one who just happened to have worked on a number of top secret programs for the British Army and the Royal Air Force. Maskelyne wrote in his 1949 book, *Magic: Top Secret*, something astounding:

"WHAT BEGAN ALMOST AS A JOKE
WAS SOON A SHARP WEAPON"

"Our men…were able to use illusions of an amusing nature in the Italian mountains, especially when operating in small groups as advance patrols scouting out the way for our general moves forward," said Maskelyne. "In one area, in particular, they used a device which was little more than a gigantic scarecrow, about twelve feet high, and able to stagger forward under its own power and emit frightful flashes and bangs. This thing scared several Italian Sicilian villages appearing in the dawn thumping its deafening way down their streets with great electric blue sparks jumping from it; and the inhabitants, who were mostly illiterate peasants, simply took to their heels for the next village, swearing that the Devil was marching ahead of the invading English."

Maskelyne concluded: "Like all tales spread among uneducated folk (and helped, no doubt, by our agents), this story assumed almost unimaginable proportions. Villages on the route of our advance began to refuse sullenly to help the retreating Germans, and to take sabotage against them; and then, instead of waiting for our troops to arrive with food and congratulations of their help, the poor people fled, thus congesting the roads along which German motorized transport was struggling to retire. The German tankmen sometimes cut through the refugees and this inflamed feeling still more, and what began almost as a joke was soon a sharp weapon in our hands which punished the Germans severely, if indirectly, for several critical weeks."

PARALLELS OF THE UNDENIABLE TYPE

Maskelyne's account caught the attention of a woman named Jean M. Hungerford. She was an expert strategist, someone who worked for the RAND Corporation, and who was the author of a paper secretly prepared for psychological warfare experts in the U.S. Air Force. Hungerford's report, titled *The Exploitation of Superstitions for Purposes of Psychological Warfare*, was published on April 14, 1950. The Air Force was highly enthused by the ways in which very strange psychological warfare could be used to confuse potential enemies, and to deceive them with bizarre scenarios. The Air Force was also very intrigued by the construction and deployment of Jasper Maskelyne's giant-sized, flashing creature.

Maskelyne said of his very own Frankenstein's Monster that it was "little more than a gigantic scarecrow" that had the ability to "stagger forward under its own power." The front-cover of Feschino's book, *The Braxton County Monster*, displays a cool, atmospheric piece of artwork. It shows a giant thing with a red head, beams of light coming from its eyes, and with the ground illuminated. Maskelyne's Devil-like beast emitted "frightful flashes and bangs." In terms of the height of the Flatwoods Monster, Feschino said it was "twelve-foot tall." Maskelyne described his crazy creation as being "twelve feet high." And, both the Italian monster and the Flatwoods Monster were seen – or, rather, were secretly tested – in wooded areas and in the vicinity of small, isolated villages and towns, just like the Rendlesham events. It seems a lot of top secret experiments of a bogus UFO nature go on in woods and forests.

TIMELINES

There's also the important matter of how all of this occurred, time-wise. It was in the latter stages of the Second World War that Jasper Maskelyne's fiendish Goliath was let loose on Italian villages. Four years after the war was over (1949), Maskelyne spilled the beans on his fantastic project in the pages of his *Magic: Top Secret Book*. One year after that, in 1950, Jean Hungerford informed the Air Force of Maskelyne's strange and highly alternative operations in Italy. And, just two years after that, we have the Flatwoods Monster appearing on the scene. Only someone in deep denial could fail to note all of the parallels that exist between the monster of those little Italian villages in the latter part of the Second World War and the "alien" that briefly terrorized the folk of Flatwoods in 1952.

We aren't quite done: there's the matter of Hungerford's report being written for psychological warfare experts in the Air Force. The U.S. Department of Defense defines psychological warfare in these words: "The planned use of propaganda and other psychological actions having *the primary purpose of influencing the opinions, emotions, attitudes, and behavior* [italics mine] of hostile foreign groups in such a way as to support the achievement of national objectives."

What we see here is that from September 1952 – when monster mayhem broke out - to December 1980, not much changed at all: it was all about using the UFO phenomenon for reasons that were almost too fantastic to comprehend. Yet, it all happened. I now have to destroy *yet another* ufological classic. I take no pleasure in doing so. Really, *I don't*. But, if we are to understand how and why we have all been so outrageously deceived for years, and with Rendlesham being the biggest example, we have to push on.

16

"CONCOCTING A SCENARIO"

In the latter part of the 1970s, journalist, UFO investigator and blogger Rich Reynolds was approached by a man named Bosco Nedelcovic, who said that he knew the real story behind one of Ufology's most alternative UFO cases of the 20th century. Nedelcovic, who died in 2000, worked for the U.S. Department of State's Agency for International Development in both Central America and South America. He also had links to the CIA. Intriguingly, Nedelcovic spent time working for the Department of Defense: it was on a 1960s-period CIA operation to infiltrate the Washington, D.C.-based Institute for Policy Studies. The IPS is a think-tank that, at the time, was heavily involved in promoting civil-rights matters and the anti-Vietnam War movement.

The *Washington Post* said in their obituary of Nedelcovic that he was also "a linguist with the American Defense College at Fort McNair and a tenacious promoter of building a Utopian society that blended elements of socialism and free market capitalism." The *Post* signed off, noting that Nedelcovic "died of prostate cancer Dec. 25 at the Northern Virginia Hospice."

"VILLAS BOAS HAD BEEN SUBJECTED TO VARIOUS DRUGS"

As for the story that Nedelcovic wanted to share with Rich Reynolds, it concerned the almost-over-the-top tale of a young Brazilian man. His name was Antonio Villas Boas. He worked on his family's farm at the time but went on to become a well-respected attorney. It was on February 22, 1958 that Villas Boas prepared for Dr. Olavo Fontes a remarkable document. Fontes, at the time, was a respected gastroenterologist at the National School of Medicine in Rio de Janeiro and a highly dedicated Flying Saucer investigator. That document told of his, Villas Boas', close encounter with an alien on October 15, 1957. But this was no sterile "take me to your leader"-style experience involving bug-eyed, spindly creatures. Nope. According to the then-twenty-three-year-old farmer, he went where, quite possibly, no man had ever gone before. That is, after being forcibly taken on-board a UFO by very human-like beings. Villas Boas proudly told Fontes he was guided to get it on with a hot E.T. babe from the great and mysterious beyond. Or, that's what certain people engaged in sophisticated mind-manipulation operations wanted Villas Boas and Fontes to *think* occurred.

"NEW FORMS OF PSYCHOLOGICAL TESTING"

For many Flying Saucer seekers now in their sixties, seventies and eighties – and who grew up with the case - the Villas Boas incident still remains a classic of its time. It's a story that is not to be, ahem, fucked with. The fact is, though, that when we address the case carefully, we *do* see a body of solid data that suggests the alien encounter was actually nothing of the sort. Let's take a look at the "UFO" that Villas Boas was taken aboard in his drugged-out state. Nedelcovic claimed it was really a military helicopter. There are very good reasons as to why we should go with Nedelcovic's claims. Take a careful look at what Villas Boas had to say about the craft he found himself on-board, and you'll see what I mean. Villas Boas said the craft was shaped "like a large elongated egg." He described it further, stating, "on the upper part of the machine there was something which was revolving at great speed and also giving off a powerful reddish light."

When the vehicle left the scene, said Villas Boas, it moved "slowly into the air until it had reached a height of some 30 to 50 meters...The whirring noise of the air being displaced became much more intense and the revolving dish began to turn at a fearful speed...At that moment, the machine suddenly changed direction, with an abrupt movement, making a louder noise, a sort of beat."

Contrary to what has been said, Villas Boas was *never* taken on-board a Flying Saucer-shaped craft. Villas Boas' own words demonstrate that. On top of that same machine was something that was "revolving at great speed." Rotor-blades? What else? *Nothing*, that's what. Then, there was the noise coming from the craft: "a sort of beat." You certainly don't have to be an aviation expert to realize that Villas Boas, even in his druggy state, had seen – and had been taken onto – a helicopter, as Nedelcovic had claimed all along.

But, what of that remarkably alluring alien who demanded a wild time in the sack?

"THIS SOUNDS LIKE KINKY SEX FROM
A PORNOGRAPHY MOVIE"

Rich Reynolds reported: "The story from Nedelcovic was that after Villas Boas had been subjected to various drugs, the part with the woman was literally acted out. So, there may have been a real woman. But in Villas Boas' case, it could have been manipulation-induced. It gave me visions of the CIA employing people of an Asian-kind of demeanor and look. It's in the realm of possibility that someone was concocting a scenario in that way."

The big question, in relation to Rich's wise words, is this: who was the girl that took Villas Boas for the "ride" of a lifetime? As for the answer, Rich was almost certainly right on target when he connected the girl to the CIA.

HOOK LINE AND SINKER

On August 31, 1977, the Pennsylvania-based *Scranton Times* ran an article titled: "CIA Used Prostitutes To Administer Drugs." One section of the article notes that the CIA "opened houses of prostitution in San Francisco and New York City with the purpose supposedly being to secretly observe how unsuspecting male customers would react to doses of LSD and other drugs that were being administered to them without their knowledge."

The story doesn't end there. The *Scranton Times* continued: "As detailed at a hearing by a Senate subcommittee on the CIA's drug and mind-bending experiments of the 1950s, a CIA agent would observe from behind a two-way mirror as prostitutes would slip their customers various chemical compounds that the agency was testing. This sounds like kinky sex from a pornography movie studio rather than a serious spying operation. Yet, we are told that it happened."

A hot hooker and LSD: put those two components together and it's no wonder Villas Boas thought he had hit the extraterrestrial jackpot. One last thing on the Villas Boas situation: Nedolcovic revealed to Rich Reynolds that the team who ran the experiment "were participating in new forms of psychological testing that would eventually be used in military contexts." We can make a *very* strong case that "psychological testing" in "military contexts" could effortlessly be applied to what happened in Rendlesham Forest more than twenty years after Villas Boas got it on in wild style.

17

"THE INJUDICIOUS USE OF MICROWAVE TECHNOLOGY"

Scoriton is an old, inviting English village that sits on the border of a huge expanse of wilderness called Dartmoor. Ancient stone circles pepper the landscape, as do Bronze Age-era remains and remnants from the Neolithic era. Dartmoor was perhaps made most famous by the fact it's where Sir Arthur Conan Doyle set much of his classic Sherlock Holmes story, *The Hound of the Baskervilles*. In 1965, the area was briefly in the local news when a strange UFO event occurred. It was an incident – or rather, a series of incidents – that, just like the Rendlesham Forest tests, turned out to be the result of classified experimentation. In this case, however, something went wrong. Fatally so.

It was on April 24, 1965 when a man named Arthur Bryant – who lived in Scoriton and who was outside at the time of his sighting – had an encounter of the close-up type. He was stunned by the sight of a Flying Saucer suspended in the sky, at a very low level and over a nearby field. Bryant was rooted to the spot – due to a combination of amazement and fear – as the strange craft suddenly descended to the ground. It's hardly surprising that Bryant was the only witness to the landing: even today the village is comprised of less than thirty houses. Also, most people would have likely been at work during the day. The stark reality suddenly hit Bryant: he was all alone with a craft – maybe even a crew - from another world.

THEY CAME IN PEACE

On reaching the strange-looking vehicle, Bryant saw a trio of entities exit from it. They looked human, but there was just something about them that made Bryant realize they weren't everyday people: their foreheads were slightly bigger than normal and they appeared to have difficulty breathing. Weirdest of all, they lacked thumbs. As for their clothing, they were identical: silver, one-piece outfits. The group from the stars slowly approached Bryant. One of them came closer still: he spoke English and claimed that he hailed from none other than the planet Venus. Not exactly the kind of thing you expect to see and hear on the average day in a tiny English village.

Incredibly, Bryant said he was taken on-board the spaceship, essentially so he could have a good look at it. No one can say the aliens weren't generous. Moments later, Bryant was motioned to leave the UFO. He did as he was told and watched as the vehicle and its crew took to the skies and vanished. It must be said that much of Bryant's story was, and still is, difficult to believe. It all sounded very much like Bryant had concocted the story after watching a couple of classic 1950s-era sci-fi movies – *The Day the Earth Stood Still* and *This Island Earth*, portions of which most definitely echoed Bryant's story.

Largely due to Scoriton being so small, it didn't take much time before all of the villagers knew of what Bryant claimed to have experienced. Soon, the local media was onto the story. Bryant's story grew even more; it was – almost inevitably - splashed on the pages of the national newspapers, too. One of those who saw the story was a woman named Eileen Buckle. She just happened to be a UFO researcher and writer – and someone who went on to write the definitive book on Bryant's claims: The *Scoriton Mystery*. It was published in 1967. It seemed to have been yet another fantastic UFO incident of the type that have been described all over the world and for decades. Except for one thing: tragedy was looming large for Bryant. It wasn't long before he died of an aggressive brain-tumor. There was, however, something else about Bryant's encounter; something that suggested strongly portions of his experience had been manufactured by intelligence agencies.

To understand the next part of the story, we must get reacquainted with Bosco Nedelcovic.

ALIENS AND AN ACCIDENTAL DEATH

Not only did Nedelcovic claim to have known just about all the skinny on the sex-filled story of Antonio Villas Boas; he also had something to say about Arthur Bryant's death. We may never know for certain if Bryant's experience really occurred as he claimed it did. Maybe it was all some kind of strange vision. Perhaps it was a hoax. Or, Bryant could have told the story *exactly* as it happened. Nedelcovic, however, asserted that U.S. Intelligence didn't really care if Bryant was telling the truth or not. What they wanted was for his story to be expanded and circulated – and to see how the story was received.

Bryant, unknown to himself, was now a targeted man. Nedelcovic said that CIA personnel achieved their goal of continuing Bryant's claims by using what were described as "visual displays, radar displacement, and artifact droppings." In simple terms, the CIA – which was said to have been the agency at the forefront of the program, Nedelcovic noted – chose to elaborate on Bryant's original story, regardless of whether it was true or false, or somewhere in between. Agents staged further incidents in and around the Bryant home; even stealthily breaking in at times when the family was out. The plot was designed to gauge the extent to which Bryant would come to believe that he was undergoing more and more alien encounters - when it was really all due to the CIA's scientists and agents. For the agency, it was an experiment. For Bryant, however, it would soon be a death sentence.

On some occasions, Bryant was said to have been exposed to "experimental drugs used to induce specific hallucinatory material." On top of that, "microwave transmissions" were used on Bryant, too. Most disturbing of all: Nedelcovic told Rich Reynolds that "the injudicious use of microwave technology" had caused Bryant to develop the tumor that quickly killed him. Supposedly, within the CIA, the operation was quietly known as "The Microwave Incident."

There is a further piece of the puzzle that needs addressing: in 1969 Robert Chapman – who was then the science correspondent for the U.K.'s *Sunday Express* newspaper – wrote a book entitled *Unidentified Flying Objects*. Chapman addressed the story of Bryant in his book, stating that "there remains a possibility" Bryant "might have had the UFO sighting planted in his mind through hypnotism." One has to wonder if Chapman, as a respected journalist working in the field of science, heard whispers of what really led to the death of Arthur Bryant.

We now come to what just might have been the most UFO-connected psychological warfare operation ever planned, and switched on, by government agents. Next to Rendlesham, that is.

KIDNAPPED ON THE ROAD

Ready to see one of the most famous alleged alien abduction incidents questioned? It's coming, anyway. It's that of Betty and Barney Hill. They were a husband and wife who, on the night of September 19, 1961, and while driving home from Canada to New Hampshire after completing a fun vacation, had a significant number of hours erased from their minds. It all happened near Indian Head, New Hampshire. It was there they saw a strange light in the sky that appeared to be carefully shadowing them from above. Concern and anxiety set in, which is no surprise. Finally, they made it home. Something very strange and disturbing happened to the Hills, but such was the state of their minds, they weren't sure what it was. But, they certainly *wanted* to know.

In the days and weeks that followed, the Hills began to experience terrifying, nerve-jangling nightmares: there were memories of having been taken on-board a UFO, and of having been subjected to intrusive and stressful medical-based experiments. Betty recalled the aliens inserted a needle into her navel. Sperm was removed from Barney, via what was termed as "a suction device." The "alien abduction" phenomenon was up and running, and the issue of "missing time" was well and truly born. The fascination the Hill's experience generated – partly due to Betty and Barney's decision to speak openly at UFO events – ultimately led to the publication in 1966 of *The Interrupted Journey: Two Lost Hours "Aboard a Flying Saucer."* It was written by a respected journalist and author, John Fuller.

The story of Betty and Barney – and of their pet dog Delsey who was also in the car at the time of the incident - still provokes interest and intrigue to this very day. It is to alien abductions what Roswell is to tales of crashed UFOs: a key case in the history of Ufology. What if, however, aliens did *not* abduct Betty and Barney?

What if – just like those who were present in Rendlesham Forest in 1980 – the pair were led to believe they had undergone something that had extraterrestrial origins, when things were actually much different?

REVEALING THE RUSE

One of those who came to believe the Hills had been subjected to an MK-ULTRA-type encounter was the late Philip Coppens. He said: "It is clear that the Hills were being monitored by USAF [U.S. Air Force] Intelligence before the encounter took place, through Major James MacDonald, who had befriended them some time earlier. Betty Hill wrote to [UFO researcher / author] Donald Keyhoe who, despite the fact that he received over a hundred letters a day, homed in on this initially unremarkable case. Within twenty-four hours, Keyhoe had arranged for the Hills to be visited by top-level scientists, including C.D. Jackson, who had previously (definitely not coincidentally) *worked on psychological warfare techniques for President Eisenhower* [italics mine]. Stretching coincidence far beyond breaking point, Jackson already knew Major MacDonald, with whom he next interviewed the Hills."

Philip continued on: "It seems that Betty and Barney Hill were at the center of a web that involved USAF Intelligence and top military experts in psychological warfare. *The evidence suggests that the Hills were the subjects – victims – of a psychological experiment* [italics mine]."

Those who believe that the Betty and Barney Hill experience was a genuine alien abduction case might very well balk at the words of Coppens. That's not a wise approach to take, though. You'll soon come to see why. Sadly, Coppens was unable to continue his work on the case for long on this topic. In 2012, he was quickly taken by a very rare form of cancer at the age of just forty-one:

Angiosarcoma. On average, it kills slightly less than two hundred people in the United States per year. Philip Coppens is gone, but the threads of his research have allowed us to take his investigations further into the associations between UFOs and mind-manipulation.

ACTIVITY BEHIND THE SCENES

In a roundabout way, the story of Betty and Barney Hill has a link to the events that occurred in Pont-Saint-Esprit on August 15, 1951. And also to MK-ULTRA. That's a jaw-dropping claim for someone to make; it is, however, absolutely true. I noted that John Fuller, in 1966, wrote a full-length book on the experiences of Betty and Barney Hill: *The Interrupted Journey*. Philip Coppens concluded that those same experiences were linked to early mind-control programs of the U.S. government.

As for Fuller, he was an intriguing character. When he died in 1990, at the age of seventy-six, the *New York Times* ran an obituary on him. It was written by a *Times* journalist, Edwin McDowell, who stated: "Mr. Fuller was sometimes criticized by reviewers for not using footnotes in his books and for what they judged was the implausibility of his topics. But as Jeff Greenfield wrote in *The New York Times Book Review* in reviewing 'The Poison That Fell From the Sky,' Mr. Fuller 'keeps raising the most unsettling of questions.' *Moreover, even before passage of the Freedom of Information Act, he had a facility for somehow obtaining Government documents* [italics mine], which he incorporated in some of his books."

The fact Fuller had a strange knack for getting his hands on official papers *prior* to FOIA passing legislation, strongly suggests he moved in intriguing places and with equally intriguing people. Powerful people, too, no doubt. As for Fuller's aforementioned 1977 book *The Poison That Fell From the Sky*, it told the story of a disastrous situation that occurred on July 10, 1976, in Seveso, Italy.

When a local chemical plant malfunctioned, the approximately 17,000 townspeople were exposed to a highly dangerous dioxin: 2, 3, 7, 8 - etrachlorodibenzodioxin. Or, in much easier terms, TCDD. Other nearby towns were hit by the dioxin, too. Studies have shown that exposure to TCDD in and around Seveso caused damage to immune-systems and nervous-systems. Cardiovascular problems surfaced, as did liver issues. It was a catastrophe of huge proportions.

JOHN FULLER, MK-ULTRA AND CONSPIRACIES

So, we have large amounts of people, in a small, old, European town, many of them severely injured as a result of the dangerous side-effects of science and technology. Does this sound familiar? It's not at all dissimilar to what happened at Pont-Saint-Esprit in 1951. The only difference was this: in one town, people had their minds blown, and in the other they were severely physically affected. I must say, John Fuller seemed to have a strange thing for disasters in small towns. Not only did he write, in 1977, *The Poison That Fell from the Sky*; Fuller also wrote a book called *The Day of St. Anthony's Fire*. The latter just happens to be one of the most authoritative books on that nightmarish 1951 incident in France that we have already addressed: the crazed events at Point-Saint-Esprit.

So, we have Fuller having written an alien abduction-themed book in 1966 (*The Interrupted Journey*, as well as two other UFO-based books: *Incident at Exeter* and *Aliens in the Skies*) and another, in 1968, on how powerful hallucinogens can wreak havoc in peoples' minds. Three decades later, Hank Albarelli made a connection between MK-ULTRA and Pont-Saint-Esprit, as we've seen. It doesn't end there. With regard to Fuller, it's about beginning.

Back in 1957, Fuller had a decidedly clandestine meeting with a Dr. Karlis Osis, as Marie Jones and Larry Flaxman note in their 2015 book, *Mind Wars*. As now-declassified CIA files on Osis reveal, he was deep into a wide range of fringe sciences and technologies, including out-of-body experiences, how to alter brain wave frequencies, the means to affect "various biophysical changes," and mind manipulation. It's no wonder Osis was also secretly consulted by the CIA's MK-ULTRA teams. Days after their first meeting, Osis introduced Fuller to a CIA man named Robert Lashbrook. It turns out Lashbrook was the very last person to see Dr. Frank Olson alive before he took that deadly, violent shove out of the Hotel Statler in Manhattan. Yes, the very same Dr. Olson who was tied to the Pont-Saint-Esprit debacle.

JOHN FULLER'S SECRET WORLD

After getting to know Fuller, Dr. Osis guardedly informed him on what was going down with the MK-ULTRA people – of the successes that had been achieved, but also of the disastrous accidents that had occurred with certain hallucinogens. Osis also made Fuller an unforeseen, amazing offer: how would he, Fuller, like to be the *very first* investigative journalist to break at least a *part* of the MK-ULTRA story to the Unites States' media? Osis was recklessly playing both sides at the same time – the government and the media - for reasons that, today, are lost and not clear. As a writer, though, Fuller immediately recognized the dollar value of the story that, potentially, just might be tossed into his lap. At the time, the mid-to-late 1950s, Fuller chose not to publish anything that might have compromised the mind-control programs that both the CIA and the U.S. Army were heavily into at that time. Clearly, however, Fuller never lost the undeniable allure of all this cloak-and-dagger activity. That is precisely why Fuller decided to write, in 1968, *The Day of St. Anthony's Fire*: he was overwhelmingly hooked on matters relative to the mysteries of the human mind. As we now know, the story that particular book told was caused by an MK-ULTRA operation that went dangerously off the rails, leaving more than a few people in asylums and with their minds in total disarray.

Osis also made a way for Fuller to speak with one Andrija Puharich. He was an American of Yugoslavian extraction, someone who was deeply interested in the mysteries of the human mind, and who, in the 1950s, just happened to work at the Edgewood, Maryland-based U.S. Army Chemical Center. The very same Edgewood Arsenal where the ball lightning-driven *Kugelblitz* program secretly ran in the 1960s; where significant research of an unethical mind-based nature was undertaken on military personnel; and whose staff secretly liaised with scientists at Porton Down, England.

From the mid-1950s, and up to at least the latter part of the 1960s, John Fuller was inextricably, and clandestinely, tied to some of the most significant players in MK-ULTRA – and in other, associated, mind-control projects. UFOs, too. And, Philip Coppens' work put psychological warfare expert C.D. Jackson right in the heart of the Hill's encounter on that dark and dangerous night home in September 1961. John Fuller is long gone and not able to defend himself. I have to say, though, that it's *very* hard to accept that Fuller – as an intelligent, investigative journalist and a skilled author – didn't make *any* of the connections between the Hill abduction and the U.S. government's mind-control operations. And particularly so as a result of his *very own* associations to the staff of MK-ULTRA. It's even harder to accept that Fuller may have been secretly, and knowingly, brought into the fold by the CIA to kick-start the alien abduction phenomenon via the very first book on the subject: *The Interrupted Journey*. I have to confess, however, that when I put all of the pieces together – not forgetting Fuller's uncanny knack of getting his hands on secret government documents - that's sure how it looks to me.

18

"EVERYONE RAN INTO THE STREET"

We saw in an earlier chapter how one of the most famous UFO abduction cases of the 1970s – that of Charles Hickson and Calvin Parker – on the Mississippi River, in October 1973, must now be viewed with great suspicion. That suspicion is due to the fact the abduction occurred close to the notorious Horn Island. It's important to note neither man can be termed liars or fantasists. Quite the opposite: the sad fact is both men were victims of their abductors, who were people and not aliens. Parker and Hickson told the story as they honestly recalled it; I am sure of that, having met Parker and having spent a weekend hanging out with him in Edinburg, Texas in 2019. But, what the pair recalled, I am also sure, was not what actually happened. There's more.

The Hickson-Parker incident happened only three months before a series of seriously strange events occurred on the Berwyn Mountains, North Wales. The Berwyns case has a connection to Porton Down, as you will soon see – and whose work and research was very similar to what had gone on at Horn Island. And six years after those Welsh mountains became famous, Rendlesham Forest became *even more* famous.

BEFORE THE FOREST THERE WERE THE MOUNTAINS

While I was researching the Rendlesham Forest story, something notable caught my attention. It was something I had never considered before: namely, the deep similarities between the 1980 incidents and a strange incident that went down six years earlier, on the night of January 23, 1974. The location? The aforementioned Berwyn Mountains, North Wales. Before I get to the Rendlesham connection to the Berwyns, I'll provide you with the background to how this equally strange series of events played out.

Without doubt, the expert on this complicated story is Andy Roberts; he's a long-time researcher of UFOs and numerous other anomalies. As for what happened in January 1974, Andy says: "Prehistoric man lived and worshipped on the mountains leaving behind him a dramatic, ritual landscape dotted with stone circles...Folklore tells us that these mountains are haunted by many types of aerial phenomena, including the spectral Hounds of Hell: those who saw them recalled how they flew through the night sky baying as though pursued by Satan himself. To the south of the Berwyn's at, Llanrhaedr-ym-Mochnant, the locals were plagued by a 'flying dragon' – intriguingly, a common name for UFOs in times gone by."

He continues: "It is against this backdrop of history and myth that on the evening of January 23, 1974 an event took place on the Berwyn Mountains that was to perplex locals and spawned a veritable cascade of rumours, culminating in a claim that, if true, would irrevocably change our view of history and make us revise our plans for the future of both our planet and our species. The claim was that a UFO piloted by extraterrestrials crashed, or was shot down, on the mountain known as Cadair Berwyn and that the alien crew, some still alive, were whisked off to a secret military installation in the south of England for study."

THE WITNESSES SPEAK

Certainly, something happened on the Berwyn Mountains at approximately 8:30 p.m. on that famous night. No one disputes that. It's the nature of the events that provoke most of the debate. Anne Williams, of Bro Diham, Landrillo, recalled: "I saw this bright light hanging in the sky. It had a long fiery tale which seemed to be motionless for several minutes, going dim and then very brilliant, like a dormant fire which keeps coming to life. It would have been like an electric bulb in shape, except that it seemed to have rough edges. Then fell somewhere behind the hills at the back of my bungalow and the earth shook."

Police Constable Gwilym Owen – off-duty at the time and knocking back a beer or a few in the local *Dudley Arms* pub - had something to say, too: "There was a great roar and a bang and the glasses shook. The sky was lit up over the mountains. The color was yellowish but other people in the valley described seeing blue lights."

Police Sergeant Gwyn Williams stated: "The walls shook and the mirror swung away from the wall," he recalled. "My first thought was that a big lorry had hit the cinema – it was that kind of a roar and bang. Everyone ran into the street." Around an hour-and-a-half later, what was described as a huge "luminous sphere," was seen by Ken Haughton at a height of around 15,000 feet in the sky. He said it seemed to fall vertically into the sea near to the town of Rhyl.

A UFO wave? That's what many thought. But, many can easily be deceived – as we have seen over and over again.

That strange lights had been seen maneuvering in the skies, and the fact the ground shook to a major degree, inevitably provoked fears that an aircraft – or, possibly, something exotic and unearthly - had crashed somewhere on the vast mountains on that winter's night. It's no surprise, then, that on the early morning of the 24[th,] a Royal Air Force emergency rescue team – operating out of the RAF Valley base – carefully scoured the Berwyns from overhead. They came away completely blank: there was no evidence of any kind of a crash having occurred. There was no debris, no fires on the mountains, and no mangled bodies, human or otherwise. The entire thing was a complete mystery.

MUCH ADO ABOUT NOTHING?

A very non-mysterious theory was put forward by the authorities: what some believed to have been a crash of something from the skies was actually an earth tremor. That does make some sense: it would have been very easy to mistake the effects of a small earthquake for a large object slamming into the ground. But, what of those lights that were seen in the skies – and at just about the same time? One theory was that they were actually the lamps of men out on the hills hunting for hares. Or, that there had been a meteorite shower – which there actually was.

Not everyone was buying into this wholly-down-to-earth picture, however. A letter was fired off to the staff of the *Wrexham Leader* newspaper by a fairly irate soul, who wrote: "Regarding your front page article '*Mystery Tremor*' in the issue of January 25, I find the explanation given absolutely ludicrous. The tremors shook houses over a 60-mile radius, and the lights were seen clearly miles away – this was reported by the national press and radio. I know nothing about 'Hare hunting' but unless the hunters use aircraft searchlights and kill their prey by lobbing a small atom bomb at them, then I fail to see how anyone can accept such an explanation."

For many, it was all a huge – and almost unique – coincidence provoked by those lamps, the meteorite shower, and an earth tremor powerful enough to shake homes and cause windows to shatter. *All* in relatively close proximity to each other. And *all* at around the same time. You can easily see why more than a few people might have chosen to use one word to describe the chaos on the mountains: "Hmmmmm."

The coincidence angle is broadly the theory that Andy Roberts goes with. Indeed, Andy wrote an entire book on the subject - and from the perspective of everything being very much UFO-absent. Its title: *UFO Down? The Berwyn Mountain UFO Crash*. It should be read by one and all. While the U.K.'s ufologists of the 1970s were briefly excited by what happened – the possibility of a UFO presence in the area, and maybe even the crash of an extraterrestrial craft – it wasn't too long before life returned to normality in the area and the incident was eventually relegated to the status of a local legend and not much more. Except, that is, for those ufologists who just couldn't let it go: a number of articles were written on the subject in the 1970s and 1980s. It wasn't until 1996, however, that the story was resurrected in a big-time, sensational fashion.

FROM THE SHADOWS COMES AN INSIDER SOURCE

We now come to what I suspect is the most significant part of this whole story – that of a connection between the Berwyns Mountains events and the experiments that occurred in Rendlesham Forest. While I think that Andy Roberts gave the UFO research community a highly plausible scenario for what happened on January 23, 1974, there is data out there that makes me conclude there were things far stranger than just meteorites in the sky on that dark night. We're talking about something that closely paralleled what was perfected at the Edgewood Arsenal in the 1960s: controlled ball lightning.

In 1996, a military whistleblower came forward, claiming aliens had crashed on the Berwyn Mountains back in January 1974. The pummeled bodies of the dead crew were said to have been secretly rushed to Porton Down for hasty examination and even hastier preservation. As is so typically often the case in such situations, the source chose not to provide his name to the UFO research community of the day. He preferred to lurk in the darkness, shrouded in mystery and intrigue. He shared his story only with Tony Dodd, who was a North Yorkshire police sergeant and UFO investigator. Dodd chose to give his talkative soldier the alias of "James Prescott," who was said by Dodd to have been long-retired from the British Army.

"I cannot name my unit or barracks, as they are still operational," Prescott told Dodd. Prescott did, though, admit that his base at the time was situated in the south-west of England, which – as the crow flies – may have placed his installation not too far from Porton Down. In a very baffling way - and although the incident on the Berwyn Mountains occurred on January 23, 1974 - Prescott and his colleagues were ordered to be on "stand-by at short notice" on January 18. That was *five days before* the Berwyns were briefly highlighted in the nation's newspapers.

Prescott got right into the heart of the story: "We then received orders to proceed with speed towards North Wales. We were halted in Chester in readiness for a military exercise we believed was about to take place. On 20 January, the communication to us was 'hot.' At approximately 20:13 hours we received orders to proceed to Llangollen in North Wales and to wait at that point."

According to Prescott there was a huge amount of "ground and aircraft activity" over and around those huge mountains. Remember, this was still January 20, according to Prescott – *three days before* the ground shook those little old villages at the foot of the mountains. Prescott said that on that same night he and his colleagues were given further orders: "We, that is myself and four others, were ordered to go to Llandderfel and were under strict orders not to stop for any civilians," claimed Prescott.

On arriving at Llandderfel - a small, Welsh village - they could see soldiers racing around. Senior officers were barking orders here, there and everywhere. Aircraft were zooming across the star-filled sky. And all of this was against a background of overwhelming darkness. Prescott and his colleagues were ordered to haul a pair of large, wooden boxes onto the back of their truck, which they did in rapid-fire time. According to Prescott: "We set off with our cargo and during the journey we stopped to get a drink. We were immediately approached by a man in civilian clothes, who produced an I.D. card and ordered us to keep moving, and not to stop until we reached our destination."

Matters got really weird, as Prescott explained to Dodd: "We were at this time warned not to open the boxes, but to proceed to Porton Down and deliver the boxes. Once inside, the boxes were opened by staff at the facility in our presence. We were shocked to see two creatures had been placed inside decontamination suits. When the suits were fully opened it was obvious the creatures were clearly not of this world and, when examined, were found to be dead. What I saw in the boxes that day made me change my whole concept of life. The bodies were about five to six feet tall, humanoid in shape, but so thin they looked almost skeletal, with a covering skin. Although I did not see a craft at the scene of the recovery, I was informed a large craft had crashed and was recovered by other military units. Sometime later we joined up with the other elements of our unit, who informed us they had also transported bodies of 'alien beings' to Porton Down, but said their cargo was still alive."

Prescott finished his sensational story to Dodd by stating this was "the only time I was ever involved in anything of this nature. This event took place many years ago and I am now retired from the Armed Forces." The tale is far from over, however. The following is a small article that I wrote for the U.K.'s UFO research community in the late 1990s. In terms of addressing the issue of James Prescott, it is still valid and informative more than two decades later. Here's how it reads:

One of the strangest – and undeniably unsavory – aspects of this affair surfaced in 1998 when rumors began circulating to the effect that the pseudonymous James Prescott was somehow connected with a very real James Prescott who lost his life in the Falklands War in 1982. It was May 17, 1982 when Staff Sergeant James Prescott of the Royal Engineers was killed while attempting to defuse a bomb on board *HMS Antelope*. He was later awarded a posthumous Conspicuous Gallantry Medal for his bravery.

According to Max Hastings and Simon Jenkins in their book, *The Battle for the Falklands*: "A broadcast from the bridge announced that the bomb-disposal team would try a new method of defusing the bomb. Prescott and Phillips detonated a small charge, then walked forward to inspect the results. As they approached, the bomb exploded. Prescott seemed to be hit by a door blown free by blast, which killed him immediately."

Needless to say, the fact that Tony Dodd was not told the tale until the mid-1990s means that the James Prescott killed in the war of the Falklands fourteen years previously could not have been Dodd's source of the story.

Moreover, a former colleague of Dodd's – who is also the editor of the newsstand publication on espionage *Eye-Spy Magazine*, Mark Birdsall - has stated that Dodd had told him that the name had *no significance at all*. And that he, Dodd, had merely conjured it up as a suitable pseudonym. In other words, the fact that there existed a *real* James Prescott in the Royal Engineers - and that Dodd decided to use that same name for his Army source - was something that amounted to nothing more than an unfortunate coincidence.

19

"IT WAS LIKE A WHITE BALL, SLOW-MOVING"

I have to admit – and to my deep chagrin – there was a time when I was a full-on believer that aliens landed at Rendlesham Forest in 1980, that a UFO came down on the Berwyn mountains in 1974, and that E.T's crashed outside of Roswell, New Mexico in July 1947. If you've read my 2005 book *Body Snatchers in the Desert*, and its 2017 sequel, *The Roswell UFO Conspiracy*, you will know that my "I want to believe" days are far behind me when it comes to Roswell – and when it comes to much of Ufology, too. Matters were very different back in 1996, however. I was certain that aliens died in the New Mexico desert, and I was quite enthused by the story of James Prescott when it surfaced more than two decades ago. I still *am* enthused by the Prescott story. Today, however, my interest in his claims are for reasons very different to those I had back in the 1990s.

One of those who shared her experiences with me about what happened in January 1974 was Anne Owen. She told me that at the time: "We had bought two, derelict, four-hundred-year-old cottages which we were converting. This was on a mountain above Trefriw and Llanrwst near the River Conwy. We'd taken a caravan up and a horse, as well, and our two children. We had a friend of ours visiting us – a lecturer and mathematician from Toronto University – and we converted a small barn into a bit of a house with a window for him. We were in the caravan with the children, as we couldn't move into the cottages yet. That night – January twenty-three – the horse was very restless, so we put him near our caravan. But later in the night he started rocking the caravan and was in a terrible state.

"Then we suddenly saw this thing outside the window. It was like a white ball, very slow-moving. It was difficult to know how far away from us it was as it was pitch black outside, but it looked about two or three feet wide. Then suddenly there was an enormous bang, absolutely colossal. At first, we thought it had hit the place where our friend was. Luckily it didn't hit him, so we weren't actually sure where it had hit. But in the morning, our friend was outside looking at a rowan tree that had been forced out of the ground. What was strangest of all was that the tree had been stripped of all its bark and had been up-rooted and thrown four hundred feet."

Anne continued: "The only other person who was local to us was an old lady who was staring at it too. Well, she came up to me and said that she'd been woken by the bang. She also lived on the mountain and had gone to her bedroom window and had seen these 'little men' that were very small and all dressed in black – about three to four foot tall. She thought, because she'd seen the military on the mountain before that this was something to do with them. But she found it rather odd that they were so small! She described a 'little gathering' of them, about four or five, very, very early in the morning and near where the tree was. But she said that they didn't look too different, only smaller.

"When she went down to the village to tell the story, everyone thought that she was mad and then when we asked her again she wouldn't talk about it anymore. Although we did know of people in Trefriw who had had their windows broken by this thing.

"But we had a group of people come from Cardiff University and they started to photograph the tree and all around it. They said they had had some instances of UFOs in the area and had been 'sent to investigate' what had taken place. This happened within one day of this taking place. They sent us a photograph that showed a white cylinder where the tree had stood and that wasn't there when the picture was taken – you couldn't see it with the naked eye. They asked us if we knew what it was, but we had no idea.

"The oddest thing of all, though, was how the people from the university knew what had happened. They were in their forties and fifties then; so they weren't students. But the day before, and the day after, this happened a weird mist came down out of nowhere. This was nothing like a normal mist and I still remember it now. I wish I had the answers to it all, but all I can do is tell you what I remember."

This account from Anne Owen has an air of the Men in Black attached to it: mysterious figures claiming to have come from a respected university, who somehow knew of the traumatic experiences of Anne Owen and her family, and who asked questions of the Owen family. In his book *UFO Down?* Andy Roberts demystifies a few tales of MIB-type activity in and around North Wales at the time. The story of Anne Owen, however, seems to me to be somewhat more mystifying and far less explainable than other Men in Black cases.

"THEY'D BEEN TAKEN TO PORTON DOWN"

There's also the fascinating story of Bob Bolton. I first interviewed him by phone, and then met him in person, in Norwich, England, in 2000. He told me: "I spent thirty years in the Royal Air Force as an aircraft engineer. I had various postings, including at Akrotiri in Cyprus, RAF Honnington, and at RAF Valley in North Wales from 1971 to 1974. My wife and her family came from Corwen. At the time the thing on the Berwyns happened, they lived up on the side of the mountain and her mom still lives there to this day. Corwen is part of the Berwyn range. From where their house is, if you walk up the path that goes behind the houses up and onto the top of the mountains, you're talking perhaps a mile and a quarter away from where it all occurred; so it's not very far away at all.

"She still remembers what happened on the night of 23 January. She said to me when I spoke to her about it just recently: 'I saw aircraft and heard aircraft shot down during the Blitz and it was like an aircraft coming down, but the sound was louder, bigger, heavier that anything you could imagine to do with an aircraft.'

"They didn't know what it was. They heard the noise first of all and ran out into the road. They weren't the only ones: all their neighbors ran out as well. It got louder and louder and louder and they couldn't see anything in the sky but then they felt the impact where the houses shook and she had things fall off the mantle-piece in the house.

"It was my wife's dad, who told me the story about bodies being found on the mountain. His name was Harold Smith. But everyone called him Mick. He had a full-time job with Vauxhall at Elsmere Port; he was a local councilor and was also a part-time Sub-Fire Officer at Corwen. One day we got talking and got on to the subject of UFOs and he said to me: 'Oh, well, you obviously don't know about the incident up on the Berwyn Mountains.'

"I first heard the story from him around 1976. At that time he only told me that bodies had been brought down from the mountain and didn't say anything more. Nothing about who brought them down or where they were taken. But from 1979 to 1982 I was posted to Germany and Mick and my wife's mother came out to stay for a month and it was here that he told us a lot more.

"I remember that the information that he told us had apparently come from another person in the North Wales Fire Service whose son was in the Army. But it's not surprising that he would have been told: Mick was a well-respected man and knew people throughout the North Wales Fire Service including at Bala and Wrexham. Mick told me that while the police weren't involved, the Army was – heavily. I can't give you an exact date when they visited and he told us this, but it was definitely between 1979 and 1982. He said that there were definitely [trucks] from Porton Down at the scene; that there was a lozenge-shaped object on the mountainside; and that bodies were taken off the mountain and driven to Porton. And to this day, his wife can also confirm that Mick told her the story about Porton Down and bodies too – either in the late 1970s or the early 1980s.

"I do remember Mick saying that when he had first told me this story in 1976, he didn't know that it was the Army who had taken the bodies off the mountain and he didn't know at the time that they'd been taken to Porton Down. So he must have learned that between 1976 and when he came to see us in Germany."

THE STORY GETS FOGGY

With that all said, let us now address my reasons for concluding that the incidents on the mountains were, collectively, an earlier incarnation of what happened six years later in Rendlesham Forest. First, we have those balls of light that seemed to have been more (or less) than meteorites, one of which Anne Owen saw at very close quarters. Her story is clearly demonstrable of that. I suspect Anne was confronted by ball lightning of the controlled type. There's also the "weird mist" that was "nothing like a normal mist" on the hills, as Anne intriguingly worded it. Researcher and writer Brian Dunning says of what was seen at Rendlesham Forest six years later: "Base personnel described the craft they pursued as metal and conical, with a bright red light above and a circle of blue lights below, and suspended in *a yellow mist* [italics mine]."

Howstuffworks wrote an article titled "The Rendlesham Forest Incident." They say: "The following evening, after observers reported strange lights, the deputy base commander, Lt. Col. Charles Halt, led a larger party into Rendlesham. There, Halt measured abnormal amounts of radiation at the original landing site. Another, smaller group, off on a separate trek through the forest, spotted a dancing red light inside *an eerily pulsating 'fog'* [italics mine]."

I have two questions for you: Is it just a coincidence that Anne Owen saw a large ball of light on her property in January 1974 and that was accompanied by a strange mist? Is it just a coincidence that the very same phenomena – a ball of light and a weird fog - was seen at Rendlesham Forest in 1980?

Maybe what was seen at both sites was not a mystifying fog but a deployed airborne hallucinogen. That might sound too "out there" for some people. I disagree. We know that Porton Down staff were heavily involved in what happened in Suffolk in 1980 – they were integral to the program. And, we've seen the lengths to which those behind the Rendlesham Forest operations went when it came to creating visions of aliens and UFOs in the woods. Perhaps, something nearly identical happened on the Berwyn Mountains and was responsible for the encounter of that old lady who saw those "little men" attired in black and "about three to four foot tall," as Anne Owen worded it. Recall that the same old lady was looking at that ball of light when she saw those diminutive extraterrestrials. And when she was likely plunged into an altered state of mind.

There's one more angle to all this that is worth addressing, as it is relevant to that strange fog seen in both Rendlesham Forest and on the Berwyn Mountains.

"A CHEMICAL FOG"

On October 6, 2017, Canada's *National Post* ran an article titled "U.S. secretly tested carcinogen in Western Canada during the Cold War, researcher finds." In part, the article states: "Between July 9, 1953 and Aug 1, 1953, six kilograms of zinc cadmium sulfide was sprayed onto unsuspecting citizens of Winnipeg from U.S. Army planes. The Army returned 11 years later and repeated the experiments in Suffield, Alta. and Medicine Hat, Alta., according to Lisa Martino-Taylor.

"Local governments had no knowledge of these experiments, according to documents obtained by Martino-Taylor, a professor of sociology at St. Louis Community College and author of *Behind the Fog: How the U.S. Cold War Radiological Weapons Program Exposed Innocent Americans*. Instead, they were fed a cover story by the Pentagon. '*In Winnipeg, they said they were testing what they characterized as a chemical fog* [italics mine] to protect Winnipeg in the event of a Russian attack," Martino-Taylor said. 'They characterized it as a defensive study when it was actually an offensive study.'"

ALMOST A THEATRICAL PERFORMANCE
FOR THE TROOPS

We need to take a deeper look at the claims of James Prescott – or whatever his real name may have been. I know from discussion and debate that many people in Ufology have overlooked – or simply don't know – the fact that although the primary event occurred on January 23, 1974, Prescott explicitly stated he and his unit were put on stand-by for something big on January *18*. That was *almost a week before* the incidents on and around those mountains erupted. And, there's the not-insignificant revelation that Prescott and his fellow soldiers were ordered to get ready for "a military exercise." This strongly suggests what happened on the Berwyn Mountains did *not* amount to a series of random, out of the blue, incidents and sightings involving meteorites or lamps. And not UFOs, either. The extensive timeframe involved in January 1974 suggests someone was carefully and quietly getting ready to implement a top secret operation; an operation that required detailed pre-planned activity on a dark night in North Wales. Just like there was a great deal of days-long planning ahead of what happened in Rendlesham Forest.

Also ripe for scrutiny are Prescott's claims that not only did he and his group drive to Porton Down, they even got to see a number of alien bodies supposedly found on the mountains. This is patently ridiculous. If creatures from another world really did meet their deaths somewhere in the mountains of North Wales in January 1974 - and were hastily driven to Porton Down – the idea that Porton Down's scientists would have casually exposed Prescott and his men to alien bodies is utterly absurd. The soldiers were never asked to put on Hazmat-type suits to protect them from what could conceivably have been deadly extraterrestrial viruses. Such a scenario defies common sense to just about the ultimate degree possible. Unless, that is, the bodies were not the real deal. They may have been sophisticated dummies, designed to help create the end game that someone dearly wanted: a manipulative ruse of massive proportions. If alien spaceships can be "created" in Rendlesham Forest, then rustling up a few extraterrestrial-looking mannequins would not have been a problem. All we can say about this particular point is that Prescott and his men were clearly *meant* to see the bodies – or the dummies. That much is obvious. And it smacks of manipulation to a huge degree. It's important to note this is not the only occasion on which government agencies have played mind-games with military personnel – and also in relation to so-called alien bodies. One example involved none other than a famous astronaut, as you will now learn.

"IT WAS A HOAX"

UFO investigator Leonard Stringfield was told of several old pieces of film that seemingly showed alien corpses. One such story came to Stringfield by "T.E." He was a young man who said that he saw just such a film in 1953 - when he was only twenty - at Fort Monmouth, New Jersey. According to what Stringfield knew, T.E. and some of his colleagues were taken to a room where they were told they were about to watch a piece of film. Stringfield wrote: "Without any briefing, the 16mm movie projector was flicked on and the film began to roll on the screen…the film showed a desert scene dominated by a silver disc-shaped object embedded in the sand…"

Stringfield continued that there "was a change of scenes." The story went on: "Now in view were two tables, probably taken inside a tent, on which, to his surprise, were dead bodies. T.E. said the bodies appeared little by human standards and most notable were the heads, all looking alike, and all being large compared to their body sizes…They looked Mongoloid." The men were advised to "think about the movie." It is no surprise at all that that was *exactly* what they did. A few days later, however, they were all told, "It was a hoax." Just like Prescott, T.E.'s words made no sense – exposing soldiers and airmen to dead aliens for no logical reason - but they definitely paralleled what Prescott said. Someone spent a great deal of time promoting the idea that both the U.K. and the U.S. governments have dead aliens in their military facilities. And just like the Rendlesham Forest case, a lot of top-secret effort went into a program that had at its heart absolute, widespread manipulation of mindsets.

Interestingly, T.E. and his colleagues were told immediately after the screening to "think about the movie." Not long later, however, they were advised: "It was a hoax." Intriguing words.

Another of those who found himself in a situation very similar to that of James Prescott was Ellison Onizuka. He was one of the astronauts tragically killed in NASA's *Challenger* Space Shuttle disaster in January 1986. It's interesting to note that a good friend of Onizuka's, Chris Coffey, has gone on record as saying Onizuka quietly told him he had seen a black-and-white film held at McClelland Air Force Base, California, in 1973 that displayed "alien bodies on a slab." It's a story UFO researcher and author Leonard Stringfield published in a 1989 report on crashed UFOs. The primary issue in all of this is *why*, exactly, Onizuka was shown the footage. There didn't seem to be any particular reason for exposing Onizuka to the film. Clearly, though, someone wanted knowledge of the footage to be known. Once more we see what is likely to have been a carefully crafted ruse to see how people can be massively manipulated.

DIVERSIONS

Bob Bolton was sure that bodies were found on the Berwyns and taken to Porton Down in January 1974. *Never once*, however, did he refer to the corpses as "alien bodies". All he knew was something mystifying happened on the hills and that bodies were brought down. The following is nothing but speculation on my part, but if the Berwyn enigma really did mirror Rendlesham, then the bodies may have been of military personnel – rather than of aliens. They may have become victims of a pre-Rendlesham-type experiment that went catastrophically wrong; something that resulted in military casualties. If so, that would definitely help to explain why the James Prescott story was pushed and rushed out in 1996: to deliberately divert the media and Ufologists away from stories of military victims. And, instead, practically force them down an avenue filled with stories of dead extraterrestrials – something that the mainstream media would likely dismiss as garbage. Thus, the truth concerning a mid-1970s-era, "pre-Rendlesham" experiment would remain buried.

Just like Rendlesham, the Berwyn Mountains incident involved fantastic visions, mysterious fog and mist that may have been evidence of hallucinogens, enchanting balls of light, Porton Down connections, top secret military experiments, and operations that were coordinated days ahead of the main event. *All* of those particular components can be found on the slopes of the ancient Berwyn Mountains and in the heart of Rendlesham Forest. Yet again, we were lied to, and blatantly deceived by skilled manipulators.

It should be clear by now that the story I have shared with you didn't begin, out of nowhere, four decades ago in those Suffolk woods. Nor did it start with the operation on the Berwyn Mountains in January 1974. It wasn't even kick-started by the events that prematurely sent poor Arthur Bryant to his grave in 1965, that terrified Betty and Barney Hill in 1961, that had Antonio Villas in a state of excitement in 1957, and that shook the good folk of Flatwoods, West Virginia in 1952. It goes right back to the latter part of the 1940s, the dawning of Ufology. That was when research into ball lightning was controversially combined with burgeoning mind-control programs – and, later, with sophisticated hologram-based technology. And, as a consequence, multiple Frankenstein's monsters were unleashed. The biggest monster of them all was Rendlesham.

AFTERWORD

In early 2020, there was an incredible development in the overall story of *The Rendlesham Forest UFO Conspiracy*. It was a very welcome, but mysterious, development that suggested not only was I on the right track; but, that I had sympathetic insiders in the U.S. government or the military who wanted the full, unexpurgated story out for everyone to see - finally. Before we get to that development, however, we need to see how the high-strangeness began and where things are at now, as our story spirals towards its end.

There is a distinct probability that none other than the late Brad Steiger – who was probably the most prodigious figure in the field of writing in the realms of conspiracies, the paranormal, UFOs – knew something of *Project Kugelblitz*. Steiger, who passed away in 2018 at the age of eighty-two, wrote more than 160 books. It is, however, just *one* of those many books we need to focus our attention on. It is *World of the Weird*, one of Steiger's lesser-known titles. It was published by Belmont Books. The book – that I had never heard of before this 2020 development occurred - contains a chapter titled "The Mystery of Lightning Balls." As can be deduced from the title of that chapter, it's a study of ball lightning.

Before we get to my role in this latest development, I'll give you some background material on Steiger's book.

"AS A WEAPON, IT WOULD BE AWESOME"

In *World of the Weird,* Steiger cited the words of Dr. Harold W. Lewis, a professor of physics at the University of Wisconsin, who said: "Any normal, cynical scientist, on hearing of ball lightning for the first time, almost instinctively places it in the category of folklore, along with flying saucers and ectoplasm. A brief survey of reported events, however, quickly convinces the skeptic that enough reputable observers have seen and possibly even photographed ball lightning to leave no doubt that the phenomenon is real, although it is rare and as yet unexplained."

It wasn't so much the mystery surrounding ball lightning that intrigued Steiger. Rather, it was the potential military application of ball lightning as a weapon. This gets to the very heart of the *Kugelblitz* operation. Steiger's book was published in 1966, having been written one year earlier, 1965. That was the same time in which the *Kugelblitz* program began in earnest.

Steiger wrote: "Recent reports of lightning balls have spurred scientists, who before simply had no use for such rare phenomena, to become very curious as to how they can reproduce such a bundle of electricity in their laboratories. The new investigations have probably not taken place only in this country. Certain information indicates that the Soviet Union is just as curious about the production and control of this phenomenon as the U.S. is."

Steiger got to the heart of the situation: "Such a concentrated ball of energy, if harnessed, could be put to hundreds of military as well as civilian uses. As a weapon, it would be awesome. It could not be shot down by a presently available firepower, and its concentrated heat could penetrate any normal armor."

It scarcely needs stating that Steiger's words practically mirror the words contained in the 1965 *Project Kugelblitz* report. Did Steiger somehow have access to the contents of the report? Did he have an insider source who helped him to expose the story? While the chances of answering those questions are slim, there is another – equally intriguing – development in all of this. It ties in with my very own research into this field. And, it brings a degree of conspiracy and inside-information into the mysterious story.

A PACKAGE ARRIVES ON MY DOORSTEP

It was not until September 2019 that I finally decided – with the 40th anniversary of the Rendlesham events coming in the following year – to go ahead and write the book that you now hold in your hands, or which you have on your Kindle. At the time, the only people who knew of the project were me and my literary agent, Lisa Hagan – who has been my agent for more than fifteen years. That's it: no one else at all. When I told Lisa of the idea for the book, she was highly enthused. A deal was made, a contract was drawn up, and the wheels began to turn, which included interviewing Ray Boeche. He became the third person to know about the planned book. My editor, Beth Wareham, was next to learn of the project. We were, then, a "Gang of four," to shamelessly hijack the name of a post-punk band of the late 1970s.

I began the actual writing of my book in late November 2019, starting with the chapter on the *Kugelblitz* controversy, and I completed the entire manuscript in the last week of April 2020. Eleven days into the writing, something very weird happened: a package was dropped off on my doorstep. I say "dropped off" because it clearly didn't come through the usual sources, such as FedEx, UPS or the Post Office. It was a manila envelope that was covered in scotch-tape – in fact, there was way more tape than was needed. My name was written on the front of the envelope with a black-marker. As for my name, it didn't just say "Nick Redfern." Rather, it said: "Nick D. Redfern." Not many know that

I have a middle name. It's David. But, whoever sent the package to me evidently *did* know. Maybe, it was done so I would realize someone knew more about me than most did. Who knows? The weirdness – and what I deduced to be strange mind-games - didn't end there, however.

A STRANGER IN THE NIGHT

I opened the envelope to find inside a first edition copy of Brad Steiger's *World of the Weird*. Within the pages was a bookmarker. It had been inserted between the very same pages of Steiger's book I referenced above: those that concerned the weaponizing of ball lightning. It was clearly a very old bookmarker – that much was evident as a result of its somewhat slightly torn, faded and creased appearance. That same bookmarker was the work of a now-closed bookstore in Minot, North Dakota called *Town Crier*. The blurb on their markers: "The place to mark for all your books, paperbacks, magazines 'n greetings cards is…Town Crier." The words "Minot, ND" on the bookmarker had been highlighted in yellow.

I thought to myself: why such highlighting on an old book-marker? In fact, why *any* kind of marker, *at all?* Well, when I saw where, precisely, the marker was placed – between the specific pages of the Steiger book concerning the utilization of ball light-ning as a weapon – I realized the book had been sent to me with a specific purpose. But, who was the sender? I had zero chance of figuring out the answer to that question. In fact, there was no sender's address on the envelope at all. There were no stamps on it, either. I could only conclude that *someone*, at an undetermined time between around midnight the night before – which was around when I went to bed - and approximately 8:00 a.m. the next morning, when I got up, had deliberately dropped the envelope outside the door of my second-floor apartment.

There was also the matter of the reference to the city of Minot on the bookmarker. Minot – the Air Force Base - you may be intrigued to know, has a notable UFO history attached to it.

STAGED EXERCISES

In the latter part of 1975, the U.S. military found itself over-whelmed by a UFO wave of epic proportions. An Air Force document – titled *Suspicious Unknown Air Activity* - states: "Since 28 Oct 75 numerous reports of suspicious objects have been received at the NORAD CC. Reliable military personnel at Loring AFB Maine, Wurtsmith AFB, Michigan, Malmstrom AFB, MT, *Minot AFB* [italics mine], ND, and Canadian forces station Falconbridge, Ontario Canada have visually sighted suspicious objects. Objects at Loring and Wurtsmith were characterized to be helicopters. Missile site personnel, security alert teams and air defense personnel at Malmstrom, Montana report an object that sounded like a jet. FAA advised there were no jet aircraft in the vicinity. Malmstrom search and height finder radars carried the object between 9500 ft. and 15,000 ft. at a speed of seven knots."

The odd situation proceeded to get even stranger: "…per-sonnel reported the object as low as 200 ft. and said that as the interceptors approached the lights went out, after the interceptors had passed the lights came on again…*Minot AFB* [italics] on 10 Nov reported that the site was buzzed by a bright object the size of a car at an altitude of 1,000 to 2,000 ft. There was no noise emitted by the vehicle."

The now-declassified papers on the Minot Air Force Base incidents show that some of the objects were characterized as helicopters. Not because of their shape, or of the beating of the rotors of a helicopter, but as a result of the capabilities of the objects: they could hover, fly forwards and backwards – all of which a helicopter can do. There was talk of some of the Minot cases having been "staged exercises" by the military itself. The goal: to determine just how quickly and efficiently the military could respond to incidents of alternative and unforeseen natures.

Some of the sightings were not of helicopters or of what one might call a flying saucer. Nope: they were described as large balls of light. In fact, not at all unlike ball lightning. It made me think that perhaps the 1975 incidents were connected to something very similar to what happened at Rendlesham Forest half a decade later. In fact, they may have been almost identical: one series of fabricated UFO events in the northern part of the United States in 1975, and another in Suffolk, England five years later on.

A FRIEND BEHIND THE CURTAINS

Steiger's words in that same book strongly suggest he knew something of the Edgewood Arsenal experiments: he was, remember, writing about all of this when staff at Edgewood were hard at work on the very same thing – and at the very same time. Someone clearly wanted me to know what Steiger learned of all this. They certainly ensured I couldn't fail to see the relevant pages: they were bookmarked. The words "Minot, ND" on the bookmarker had been highlighted in yellow. And, Minot Air Force Base had been the site of a wave of unexplained phenomena in 1975 that mirrored what went down in Rendlesham Forest: (A) military personnel in a state of concern; and (B) strange phenomena seen over a strategic military installation.

Did I have my very own "Deep Throat?" One who, in a very odd way, tried his or her best to tell me exactly what I needed to know? Was someone trying to help me make a solid case for what happened in Rendlesham Forest? I think that's precisely what happened. An additional thing on all of this: if you are acquainted with my 2018 book, *The Black Diary*, you will recall that I detailed a near-identical situation – of a package dropped on my doorstep and under very strange circumstances – that occurred slightly more than two-and-a-half-years earlier. Someone had been keeping an eye on me. They still seem to be doing so now. And they still want the complete story of what happened in Rendesham Forest in December 1980 to be blown wide open.

The story is clearly not over. And I have every intention of continuing my quest for the full truth of what *really* happened in Rendlesham Forest.

BIBLIOGRAPHY

Note: All links were correct at the time of writing

"1977 Senate MKULTRA Hearing: Appendix A."
http://www.druglibrary.org/schaffer/history/
e1950/mkultra/AppendixA.htm. 2019.

"A coast full of secrets, Shingle Street, Suffolk."
https://www.theguardian.com/travel/2009/jun/08/
shingle-street-walking-guide-suffolk. June 8, 2009.

Albarelli, Jr., H.P. *A Terrible Mistake: The Murder of
Frank Olson and the CIA's Secret Cold War Experiments*.
Walterville, OR: Trine Day LLC, 2009.

Amos, Jonathan. "Ball lightning 'may explain UFOs.'"
https://www.bbc.com/news/science-environ-
ment-11877842. December 1, 2010.

Anderson, Paul Scott. "Has the ball lightning mystery
been solved?" https://earthsky.org/earth/ball-light-
ning-lightning-atmosphere-earth-optik. June 14, 2019.

"Andrija Puharich." https://en.wikipedia.
org/wiki/Andrija_Puharich. 2020.

Atlas Obscura. "The Hallucinations of Pont-Saint-Esprit: A small town hallucinates en masse – Bad bread, or CIA science project?" https://www.atlasobscura.com/places/the-hallucinations-of-pont-saint-esprit-pont-saint-esprit-france. 2020.

BBC. "Porton Down – The Unwitting Victims." http://www.bbc.co.uk/insideout/west/series1/porton-down.shtml. October 28, 2002.

BBC. "Rendlesham Forest UFO sighting 'new evidence' claim." https://www.bbc.com/news/uk-england-suffolk-33447592. July 13, 2015.

Beabey, Keith. "UFO Lands in Suffolk – and that's Official." *News of the World*. October 2, 1983.

"Binary Code." https://www.techopedia.com/definition/17052/binary-code. October 31, 2018.

Bowen, Charles (editor). *The Humanoids: A Survey of Worldwide Reports of Landings of Unconventional Aerial Objects and Their Occupants*. Chicago, IL: Henry Regnery Company, 1969.

"British forces overseas posting." https://www.gov.uk/guidance/british-forces-overseas-posting-dhekelia-cyprus. May 21, 2013.

Bruni, Georgina. *You can't Tell the People: The Definitive Account of the Rendlesham Forest UFO Mystery*. London, U.K.: Sidgwick & Jackson, Ltd., 2000.

Buckle, Eileen. *The Scoriton Mystery: Did Adamski Return?* London, U.K.: Neville Spearman, 1967.

Butler, Brenda, Street, Dot and Randles, Jenny. *Sky Crash*. London, U.K.: Grafton Books, 1986.

Carter, Maria. "The Eerie Story Behind the Small Town Everyone Is Flocking to for the Eclipse This Summer." https://www.countryliving.com/life/a44064/eclipseville-hopkinsville-ky-history/. July 21, 2017.

Cashman, John. *The LSD Story*. Greenwich, CT: Fawcett Publications, Inc., 1966.

Chapman, Robert. *UFO: Flying Saucers over Britain?* London, U.K.: Granada Publishing, Ltd., 1981.

"CIA Used Prostitutes to Administer Drugs." *Scranton Times*. August 31, 1977.

Clarke, David & Roberts, Andy. *Out of the Shadows: UFOs, the Establishment & the Official*

Cover-Up. London: Judy Piatkus (Publishers) Ltd., 2002.

Clarke, David and Anthony, Gary. "The British MoD Study: Project Condign." https://pdfs.semanticscholar.org/1bcb/b230b57f1e1169190ad34d51d5d59480dbe7.pdf. 2020.

Clarke, Dr. David. "The Rendlesham Files." http://drdavidclarke.blogspot.com/p/rendlesham-files.html. 2010.

Collins, Tony. *Open Verdict: An Account of 25 Mysterious Deaths in the Defense Industry*. London, U.K.: Sphere Books, Ltd., 1990.

"Condign Report," http://www.uk-ufo.org/condign/. 2020.

Coppens, Philip. "The Pied Pipers of the CIA." https://www.eyeofthepsychic.com/ufo_ciapipers/. 2020.

Correspondence between Nick Redfern and Georgina Bruni, 1998-2000.

"David Bohm, wholeness and the generative orders." https://continuumcenter.net/BP/BPDavidBohm.pdf. 2020.

"Dr. Karlis Osis." https://www.cia.gov/library/readingroom/docs/CIA-RDP96-00788R002000240004-1.pdf. October 3, 1979.

Dudding, George. *The Kelly-Hopkinsville UFO and Alien Shootout.* CreateSpace Independent Publishing Platform. January 5, 2015.

"Eugene Poteat." https://www.iwp.edu/faculty/eugene-poteat/. 2020.

Evans, Rob. "MI6 ordered LSD tests on servicemen." https://www.theguardian.com/science/2005/jan/22/uknews1. January 22, 2005.

Fawcett, Lawrence & Greenwood, Barry J. *Clear Intent: The Government Coverup of the UFO Experience.* Englewood Clifs, NJ: Prentice-Hall. Inc., 1984.

Fedaie, Deana. "Long-Term Effects of Lysergic Acid Diethylamide (LSD) Use and Potential Medicinal Uses." https://edspace.american.edu/df1092a/wp-content/uploads/sites/808/2016/10/Long-TermEffectsofLysergicAcidDiethylamideLSDUseandPotentialMedicinalUses-2.pdf. 2020.

Feschino, Frank C., Jr. *The Braxton County Monster: The Cover-Up of the 'Flatwoods Monster' Revealed.* Lulu Enterprises. 2012.

"Former Combat Support Building (Building 273), Greenham Common." https://historicengland.org. uk/listing/the-list/list-entry/1419547. 2020.

Fortwiki. "Edgewood Arsenal." http://www. fortwiki.com/Edgewood_Arsenal. 2020.

Fuller, John G. *The Interrupted Journey: Two Lost Hours "Aboard a Flying Saucer."* NY: The Dial Press. 1966. NY: Berkley Books, 1979.

Fuller, John G. *The Poison That Fell from the Sky.*

Godfrey, Linda S. *Hunting the American Werewolf.* Madison, WI: Trails Books, 2006.

Government Accountability Office. "Chemical and Biological Defense." https://www.gao. gov/assets/250/242280.html. May 2004.

"RAF Greenham Common." https://en.wikipedia. org/wiki/RAF_Greenham_Common. 2020.

Halt, Charles. United States Air Force Memorandum. January 13, 1981.

Hastings, Max and Jenkins, Simon. *The Battle for the Falklands.* NY: W. W. Norton & Company, 1984.

Henderson, Neil. "UFO files reveal 'Rendlesham incident' papers missing.'" https://www.bbc. com/news/uk-12613690. March 3, 2011.

"Highpoint Prison." https://www.gov.uk/ guidance/highpoint-prison. 2020.

History Channel. *UFO Hunters*. "Military vs. UFOs." February 27, 2008.

"HM Prison Blundeston." https://www.wikiwand.com/en/HM_Prison_Blundeston. 2020.

"HM Prison Warren Hill." https://en.wikipedia.org/wiki/HM_Prison_Warren_Hill. 2020.

"Home Office – About Us." https://www.gov.uk/government/organisations/home-office/about. 2020.

"HMP and YOI Hollesley Bay." http://www.justice.gov.uk/contacts/prison-finder/hollesley-bay. 2020.

Hungerford, Jean M. "The Exploitation of Superstitions for Purposes of Psychological Warfare." https://www.rand.org/content/dam/rand/pubs/research_memoranda/2008/RM365.pdf. April 14, 1950.

"Ian Ridpath." https://www.amazon.com/Ian-Ridpath/e/B001IYV8LC?ref=sr_ntt_srch_lnk_1&qid=1585600268&sr=1-1

Jones, Marie and Flaxman, Larry. *Mind Wars: A History of Mind Control, Surveillance, and Social Engineering by the Government, Media, and Secret Societies*. Pompton Plains, NJ: New Page Books, 2015.

Keel, John. *The Mothman Prophecies*. NY: E.P. Dutton & Co., Inc., 1975.

Keith, Jim. *Mind Control and UFOs*. Kempton, IL: Adventures Unlimited Press, 2005.

"Kentucky Goblins." https://themothman.fan-dom.com/wiki/Kentucky_Goblins. 2020.

Khatchadourian, Raffi. "Operation Delirium: "Decades after a risky Cold War experiment, a scientist lives with secrets." https://www.newyorker.com/maga-zine/2012/12/17/operation-delirium. December 10, 2012.

Klein, Christopher. "Why is the day after Christmas called Boxing Day?" https://www.history.com/news/why-is-the-day-after-christmas-called-boxing-day. August 22, 2018.

Lemm, Elaine. "What is Boxing Day and How Did It Get Its Name?" https://www.thespruce.com/what-is-boxing-day-435060. January 13, 2020.

"LSD – Testing On British Marines." https://www.you-tube.com/watch?v=KWodyapGNxI. January 23, 2012.

Lusher, Adam. "The bizarre true story of when the UK military tested LSD on Royal Marines." https://www.independent.co.uk/news/uk/home-news/lsd-video-por-ton-down-chemical-weapons-experiments-trials-uk-mili-tary-army-marines-sixties-acid-a8366906.html. May 24, 2018.

Lyttle, W.B. & Wilson, C.E. *Survey of Kugelblitz Theories For Electromagnetic Incendiaries.* U.S. Army Edgewood Arsenal, Chemical Research and Development Laboratories. December 1965.

Ferreira, Victor. "U.S. secretly tested carcinogen in Western Canada during the Cold War, researcher finds." https://nationalpost.com/news/canada/u-s-se-cretly-tested-carcinogen-in-western-canada-dur-ing-the-cold-war-researcher-discovers. October 6, 2017.

"How does radar work?" https://www.abc.net.au/science/
articles/2014/03/17/3964782.htm. March 17, 2014.

Maskelyne, Jasper. *Magic: Top Secret.* London,
U.K.: S. Paul Publishers, 1949.

McDowell, Edwin. "John Fuller, 76, Playwright, Dies:
Wrote Books on the Unexplained." https://www.nytimes.
com/1990/11/09/obituaries/john-fuller-76-playwright-dies-
wrote-books-on-the-unexplained.html. November 9, 1990.

Medical News Today. "The effects and hazards of LSD."
https://www.medicalnewstoday.com/articles/295966. 2020.

Medscape. "3-Quinuclidinyl Benzilate Poisoning."
https://emedicine.medscape.com/arti-
cle/833155-overview. February 13, 2019.

"Melpar." https://en.wikipedia.org/wiki/Melpar. 2020.

Melton, Keith and Wallace, Robert. *The Official CIA Manual of
Trickery and Deception.* NY: William Morrow Paperbacks, 2010.

Minot Memories. "1980 - Business." http://www.minotmem-
ories.com/2014/01/980-business.html. January 28, 2014.

"Mystery Tremor." *Wrexham Leader.* January 25, 1974.

National Archives. File number: AIR 20/9320.

National Trust. "After 1945 – rockets and
long range radar." https://www.nationaltrust.
org.uk/orford-ness-national-nature-reserve/
features/after-1945---rockets-and-radar.

National Trust. "History of AWRE on Orford Ness." https://www.nationaltrust.org.uk/orford-ness-national-nature-reserve/features/history-of-awre-on-orford-ness. 2020.

Nicholls, John. "A Middle East war story." http://testimony-magazine.com/back/apr2007/nicholls2.pdf. April 2007.

Noyes, Ralph. *A Secret Property*. London, U.K.: Quartet Books, Ltd., 1985. "Obituaries." https://www.washingtonpost.com/archive/local/2000/01/02/obituaries/8280 8d24-fc2f-4a80-b777-e638e1bbc00c/. January 2, 2000.

Oliver, J.R. Letter to Timothy Good, October 1991.

"Operation Paperclip." http://www.operationpaperclip.info/. 2016.

Parker, Calvin. *Pascagoula – The Closest Encounter: My Story*. West Yorkshire, U.K.: Flying Disk Press, 2018.

Parry, Gareth. "Peace Women Fear Electronic Zapping at Base." *Guardian*, March 10, 1986.

Penniston, Jim & Osborn, Gary. *The Rendlesham Enigma: Book 1: Timeline*. Independently Published, 2019.

Pilkington, Mark. *Mirage Men: An Adventure into Paranoia, Espionage, Psychological Warfare, and UFOs*. NY: Skyhorse Publishing, 2010.

Pope, Nick, Burroughs, John and Pennistion, Jim. *Encounter in Rendlesham Forest*. NY: Thomas Dunne Books, 2014.

Pope, Nick. "Project Condign." http://www.nick-pope.net/project-condign.htm. May 15, 2006.

Pope, Nick. *Operation Lightning Strike*. London, U.K.: Thistle Publishing, 2015.

Pope, Nick. *Operation Thunder Child*. London, U.K. Thistle Publishing, 2015.

Poteat, Gene. "Stealth, Countermeasures, and ELINT, 1960-1975." *Studies in Intelligence*. No. 1. https://www.cia.gov/library/readingroom/docs/stealth_%20count.pdf.1998.

Project 1947. "UFO Reports -1947." https://www.project1947.com/fig/1947a.htm. 2020.

"Project Grudge: American UFO Panel." https://www.britannica.com/topic/Project-Grudge. 2020.

"RAF Bentwaters/Woodbridge History." https://www.usafpolice.org/bentwaterswoodbridge-history.html. 2020.

Randerson, James. "Could we have hitched a ride on UFOs?" https://www.theguardian.com/science/2007/feb/22/freedomofinformation.it. February 22, 2007.

Randles, Jenny. *From out of the Blue: The Incredible UFO Cover-Up at Bentwaters NATO Air Base*. New Brunswick, NY: Global Communications, 1991.

Randles, Jenny. *UFO Crash Landing? Friend or Foe?* London, U.K.: Cassell PLC, 1998.

Redfern, Nick. *A Covert Agenda: The British Government's UFO Top Secrets Exposed*. London, U.K.: Simon & Schuster, 1997.

Redfern, Nick. "Aliens: Us from a Future Time?" https://mysteriousuniverse.org/2018/05/aliens-us-from-a-future-time/. May 6, 2019.

Redfern, Nick. Interview with Anne Owen, August 11, 2000.

Redfern, Nick. Interview with Bill Maguire, March 14, 1998.

Redfern, Nick. Interview with Bob Bolton, November 14, 2000.

Redfern, Nick. Interview with Matthew Williams, January 17, 1997.

Redfern, Nick. Interview with Matthew Williams, June 14, 1997.

Redfern, Nick. Interview with Nick Pope, January 22, 1997.

Redfern, Nick. Interview with Nick Pope, March 29, 1994.

Redfern, Nick. Interview with Nick Pope, October 10, 1998.

Redfern, Nick. Interview with Paul Greensill, July 24, 1995.

Redfern, Nick. Interview with Ray Boeche, January 10, 2020.

Redfern, Nick. Interview with Rich Reynolds, June 23, 2009.

Redfern, Nick. "The Multiple Mysteries of Rendlesham Forest." *Mysterious Universe*. https://mysteriousuniverse.org/2017/12/the-multiple-mysteries-of-rendlesham-forest/. December 21, 2017.

Redfern, Nick. "The Mysterious UFO-Helicopter Wave of 1975." https://jimharold.com/mysterious-ufo-helicopter-wave-1975/. March 24, 2016.

Redfern, Nick. *The Slenderman Mysteries: An Internet Urban Legend Comes To Life*. Newburyport, MA: Red Wheel/Weiser, LLC, 2017.

Redfern, Nick. "Project Kugelblitz." http://www.forteantimes.com/features/articles/2170/project_kugelblitz.html. December 30, 2009.

"Rendlesham Forest." https://www.forestryengland.uk/rendlesham-forest. 2020.

"Rendlesham Incident: A Test of Virtual Reality Projectors (Jacques Vallee)." http://www.abovetopsecret.com/forum/thread646674/pg1. January 3, 2011.

Reynolds, Rich. "The Carlos Alberto Diaz abduction, not unlike the Antonio Villas Boas episode." https://ufocon.blogspot.com/2011_09_12_archive.html. September 12, 2011.

Ridpath, Ian. "The Rendlesham UFO witness statements." http://www.ianridpath.com/ufo/rendlesham2b.htm. January 2011.

Ridpath, Ian. "Transcript of Col. Halt's Tape." http://www.ianridpath.com/ufo/halttape.htm. 2020.

Rigby, Nic. "Was WWII mystery a fake?" http://news.bbc.co.uk/2/hi/uk_news/england/2243082.stm. September 9, 2002.

Rinde, Meir. "Stranger Than Fiction." https://www.sciencehistory.org/distillations/stranger-than-fiction. December 2, 2015.

Roberts, Andy. *Albion Dreaming: A popular history of LSD in Britain.* London, U.K.: Marshall Cavendish, Ltd., 2008.

Roberts, Andy. *UFO Down? The Berwyn Mountain UFO Crash.* Woolsery, U.K.: Fortean Words, 2010.

Robbins, Peter. *Halt in Woodbridge: An Air Force Colonel's Thirty-Eight-Year Fight to Silence an Authentic UFO Whistle-Blower.* Published by Peter Robbins, 2015.

Robinson, Ben. *The Magician: John Mulholland's Secret Life.* Lybrary.com. 2008. "Roman-à-clef." https://grammarist.com/usage/roman-a-clef/. 2020.

Rose, Norman. *Twin Bases Remembered: History of RAF Bentwaters and Woodbridge.* Published by Norma Rose, 2005.

Shachtman, Noah. "CIA's Lost Magic Manual Resurfaces." https://www.wired.com/2009/11/cias-lost-magic-manual-resurfaces/. November 24, 1989.

Smith, Harrison. "James Ketchum, who conducted mind-altering experiments on soldiers, dies at 87." https://www.washingtonpost.com/local/obituaries/james-ketchum-who-conducted-mind-altering-experiments-on-soldiers-dies-at-87/2019/06/04/7b5ad322-86cc-11e9-a491-25df61c78dc4_story.html. June 4, 2019.

Smith, Lieutenant, H.W. and G. W. Towles. *Project Grudge Technical Report.* No. 102-AC 49/15-100, Air Materiel Command, August 1949.

Stacy, Dennis. "Like Ball Lightning: In Memory of Ralph Noyes." 2020. https://www.anomalist.com/milestones/noyes.html.

Steiger, Brad. *World of the Weird.* NY: Belmont Books, 1966.

Stringfield, Leonard H. *UFO Crash / Retrievals: is the Coverup Lid Lifting? Status Report V.* Cincinnati, OH: Self-published, 1989.

Taylor, Philip. "The Mystic and the Spy: Two Early British UFO Writers." http://magonia.haaan.com/1997/the-mystic-and-the-spy-two-early-british-ufo-writers/. January 11, 1997.

"The Great Storm of 1987." https://www.ipswich-star.co.uk/storms-1987-2-12363. 2020.

"The Rendlesham Forest Incident." https://science.howstuffworks.com/space/aliens-ufos/rendlesham-forest-incident.htm. 2020.

"The Rendlesham Forest Incident: The Halt Tape." https://www.youtube.com/watch?v=YZZtidhZbcE. July 24, 2015.

"The Royal Air Force in Watton." http://www.historyofwatton.org.uk/raf/briefhistory.htm. 2020.

"The War Magician: Jasper Maskelyne's clever illusions helped win WWII." https://www.magictricks.com/war-magician.html. 2020.

Thomson, Mike. "Pont-Saint-Esprit poisoning: Did the CIA spread LSD?" https://www.bbc.com/news/world-10996838. August 23, 2010.

U.S. Department of Veteran Affairs. "Edgewood / Aberdeen Experiments." https://www.publichealth.va.gov/exposures/edgewood-aberdeen/index.asp. 2020.

Roberts, Andy and Clarke, David. *UFO Brigantia*. No. 41, May 1991.

UFO Magazine, September / October, 1996.

Uman, Martin A. "Periodically I hear stories about ball lightning. Does this phenomenon really exist? Could a ball of plasma remain stable for several seconds as some researchers have claimed?" https://www.scientificameri-can.com/article/periodically-i-hear-stori/. July 18, 1997.

"United States Senate Committee on Armed Services: History." https://www.armed-services.senate.gov/about/history. 2020.

"US Military Bases in the United Kingdom." https://militarybases.com/overseas/united-kingdom/. 1998.

Warren, Larry & Robbins, Peter. *Left at East Gate: A First-Hand Account of the Rendlesham Forest UFO Incident, its Cover-Up, and Investigation.* NY: Cosimo. 2005.

Webster, Squadron Leader E.E. Letter to Nick Redfern, October 25, 1988.

Weinberger, Sharon. "Mind Games New on the Internet: a community of people who believe the government is beaming voices into their minds. They may be crazy, but the Pentagon has pursued a weapon that can do just that." https://www.washingtonpost.com/archive/lifestyle/magazine/2007/01/14/mind-games-span-classbankheadnew-on-the-internet-a-com-munity-of-people-who-believe-the-government-is-beam-ing-voices-into-their-minds-they-may-be-crazy-but-the-pen-tagon-has-pursued-a-weapon-that-can-do-just-that-span/a0d09db6-d7aa-4fcd-a829-2a3ebc56df9d/. January 14, 2007.

Wheatley, Dennis. *Star of Ill-Omen.* London, U.K.: Arrow Books, Ltd., 1971.

"When The British Army Tried LSD." https://www.forces.net/services/tri-service/when-british-army-tried-lsd. June 3, 2015.

"Who is the Rendlesham Forest Whistleblower?" https://www.facebook.com/UfoTruthMagazine/posts/who-is-the-rendlesham-forest-whistleblowerthe-first-thing-to-say-about-the-rendl/1205222576180507/. January 2, 2017.

Wood, Robert M. *Alien Viruses: Crashed UFOs, MJ-12, & Biowarfare*. Rochester, NY: Richard Dolan Press, 2013.

Zimmerman, David. "The Tizard Mission and the Development of the Atomic Bomb." *War in History*. Vol. 2, No. 3. November 1995. https://www.jstor.org/stable/26004450?seq=1.

ACKNOWLEDGMENTS

I would like to offer my sincere thanks to my agent, friend and publisher, Lisa Hagan; my editor and co-publisher, Beth Wareham; book-designer, Simon Hartshorne; Rich Reynolds, for all his work on the Antonio Villas Boas case; and Ray Boeche, for sharing his time to discuss his research into the Rendlesham Forest mystery.

ABOUT THE AUTHOR

Nick Redfern is the author of more than 60 books on UFOs, the Loch Ness Monster, Bigfoot, zombies, and Hollywood scandal. His books include *Flying Saucers from the Kremlin*; *The Roswell UFO Conspiracy*; *Women in Black*; *Men in Black*; *Nessie*; *Chupacabra Road Trip*; *The Black Diary*; and *365 Days of UFOs*. He is a regular on the Travel Channel's show, *In Search of Monsters*. Nick has also appeared on the BBC's *Out of This World*; the SyFy Channel's *Proof Positive*; the History Channel's *Monster Quest*, and *America's Book of Secrets;* the National Geographic Channel's *Paranatural*; and MSNBC's *Countdown* with Keith Olbermann. Nick lives in Arlington, Texas.

He can be contacted at his blog: http://nickredfernfortean. blogspot.com

Printed in Great Britain
by Amazon

58160662R00129